Get Off
the Best-Stressed
List!

STRATEGIES FOR
SIMPLIFYING LIFE

Jo Ann Larsen
and Artemus Cole

SHADOW MOUNTAIN

Library of Congress cataloging number 135045

ISBN 1-57345-816-3

Printed in the United States of America   72082-6713

10   9   8   7   6   5   4   3   2   1

To my miracle children, sent down from angel places,
who are an ever-present comfort and blessing.
Jo Ann Larsen

To my kids. The best stress relief in my life was hearing
you say, "I love you, Daddy." You made
me feel drop-dead gorgeous!

Artemus Cole

*"It's that stressed-out pair of Larsen
and Cole—shall I call security?"*

Contents

Introduction . . . . *ix*

Chapter 1
Put Family First *1*

Chapter 2
Make Home a Haven *15*

Chapter 3
Enhance Marriage *31*

Chapter 4
Stretch Your Self *49*

Chapter 5
Go with the Flow *61*

Chapter 6
Quit Complaining *77*

Chapter 7
Take Responsibility *87*

Chapter 8
Avoid Emotional Collisions *97*

Chapter 9
Curb Anger in Traffic *103*

Chapter 10
Control Temper Tantrums *111*

Chapter 11
Diffuse Criticism *120*

Chapter 12
Reduce Troubles *130*

Chapter 13
Challenge Worries *143*

Chapter 14
Unclutter Your Life *150*

Chapter 15
Become Stress Hardy *162*

Chapter 16
Bargain without Bickering *176*

Chapter 17
Communicate Effectively *185*

Chapter 18
Relax *193*

Chapter 19
Seek Solitude *209*

Chapter 20
Engineer Your Life *222*

Chapter 21
Count Your Blessings *234*

Sources *243*

Introduction

Was it just yesterday that your underwear shrunk, your car almost ran out of gas, it poured rain, the only parking spot available was three blocks away, the wind blew your umbrella inside out, and then you woke up?

If life's little annoyances—even just living—stress you out, you're probably on today's best-stressed list. To determine your eligibility, consider these criteria:

You know you're on the list when:

> The amount of sleep you require is usually ten
> minutes more.
>
> You hear your mouth say yes when your brain
> says no.
>
> You bite off more than you can chew, and you
> haven't even opened your mouth yet.
>
> You can't remember what day it is, what
> month it is, or your first name.

Being on the best-stressed list isn't fun. Healthy. Or wise. But most of us are eligible for membership at one time or another. In the midst of today's "hurry" epidemic, we chronically check our watches, pace before meetings, and fidget in elevators. Hassled by the clock and oppressed by urgency, we're driven by a sense of "no time." And when some obstacle gets in the way of running life's race, we may have meltdowns.

In our hurry, we say we don't have enough time. But the truth is, we simply don't have enough quality time: no time without stress, deadlines, or crises; no time where life slows to a stroll down a country lane; no time to savor little pleasures.

If we are fortunate, we realize the good things in life are not rare or costly. They are life's commonplaces: a child's smile; a sky full of clouds; flowers at our feet. They are the things money can't buy and hurrying won't secure.

It's inherent to pursue the big, the fast, and the expensive. Yet only simple, unencumbered living allows us to experience life and to live harmoniously with ourselves. Thus, this book offers myriad strategies for simplifying life across multiple dimensions of living.

To opt for simpler living and get off the best-stressed list, forge ahead, find a relaxing spot, and sample an extensive buffet of humor-spiced remedies. Quell your appetite but remember buffet etiquette: (1) you don't have to eat anything you don't like and (2) you get to taste anything that looks good.

So laugh along. Munch up. Simplify life. Live long and stress less.

CHAPTER 1

Put Family First

Strengthening families strengthens the human spirit, soothes hearts, and salves souls, thus reducing personal stress. So to shore up your family, consider these possibilities:

Take charge. First, take charge of your family. As a couple, consider yourselves an executive committee. (If you're a single-parent family, consider yourself a committee of one.) As executives, charge yourself with assuring that your family gets ample time, energy, and resources.

"Howard, you've already picked the college, the vocation, and the investment programs for our four kids. Isn't that kind of heavy for a first date?"

"George, I think we're a little too office oriented!"

Budget time. In taking charge, budget your time just as you do your money. Only so many dollars exist in your financial budget. Similarly, only so many minutes, hours, and days exist in your time budget. Make your time, as well as your dollars, count.

Schedule. Hold weekly meetings to reserve quality time for your family. Then, and only then, allocate adjustable and discretionary time. Use large X's on a calendar to block out family time. You may want to plan a whole year ahead for family vacations, school, or other holidays. Protect family time as you would any significant work commitment. Learn to tell others, "I wish I could but that's our family time."

Structure. Most often parents can reduce family stress by establishing structure. Across the board, kids are creatures of habit and thrive on routine. When they realize a routine is here to stay, kids will soon accept that routine, depend on it, and take comfort in the security they derive from pre-dictability.

Make dinnertime a family affair. Do your best to have meals together as often as possible and, in particular, make dinnertime a time of family bonding. Share interesting events of the day, funny stories or cartoons, pleasant experiences, even embarrassing moments.

Dinnertime offers a creative opportunity to foster "low-risk" family communication. Parents can specify that table talk must be positive and pleasant. Initially, this rule could be reinforced in the form of a game: First, dispense ten tokens to each family member with the lighthearted charge that any negativity warrants a forfeiture of a token. After dinner, the member with the most remaining tokens is rewarded, perhaps with a ticket pass drawn from a container promising, "One trip to the library," "One milkshake," "One free ride to school," "One movie ticket," "One dollar," and so on. Every night, assign a different family member to monitor the conversation and make non-negotiable judgments regarding whether tokens are due.

Dinnertime is also a prime time to establish that mistakes are to be treated benignly and with a light touch. Accomplish this by freely relating times during your day when you may

"George!"

have erred or tell stories of times when you were less than perfect and made mistakes or learned something important.

Establish bedtime rituals. Spend time at your children's bedside. Tuck them in, tell stories, give backrubs. Ask about their days. Encourage conversation by posing such open-ended questions as: If you had three wishes, what would you wish for? What thing is most important to you? What really annoys you? What is your biggest worry? What is your favorite thing to do?

Revive the story hour. As an active alternative to passive television viewing, online time, and computer games, revive

"Dad's bedtime stories always have some snoring in them."

the story hour. Even a few minutes a day can build language skills and introduce a new world of adventure. When grandparents become involved, reading can bind generations.

Story time doesn't have to be at bedtime. Nor does story time need to be limited to young children. Everyone enjoys a good story. Make family gatherings memorable for all ages by sharing short stories, newspaper clippings, cartoons—anything you find humorous, inspiring, entertaining. Have an occasional "Story night," where family members progressively add to a silly or funny story.

Use driving time. Increase quality time by using driving time, usually the most concentrated time parents have with kids, to just talk or laugh and have fun together.

Spend one-on-one time. Overall family closeness hinges on the health of each relationship in the family unit.

"John! You don't 'downsize' families!"

Encourage parent-child linking by finding frequent times to be alone with each child. You can do this while you clean the garage or rake leaves; work time is valuable together time.

Create family projects. Cultivate a vegetable garden, organize a box of old snapshots into a family album, or make bread from scratch.

Exercise. Teach children to keep their bodies strong

"Good heavens, Martha—can't he learn how to eat first?"

"Helen, I think you've been in the kitchen too long!"

through daily exercise. As a family, participate in physical activities such as jogging, walking, playing tennis, golfing, and so on.

Assign tasks. Divide up family tasks—doing dishes, mowing lawns, tidying rooms, and other household cleaning tasks. Post a task list and rotate assignments. Increase overall kid cooperation by consistently expressing appreciation for effort. At other times, generously and graciously respond

"It's going to be a great vacation if we can get inside the car!"

when kids ask for assistance. Hearing parents say, "I'd love to help you" provides a model for children and promotes willing involvement in task completion.

Be spontaneous. Squeeze in special moments through-out the day and week. A quick jaunt for a root beer float, a picnic in the park, a nature ride, or a walk outdoors to see the stars can be fun ways to relieve stress while nurturing your children's sense of wonder and curiosity.

Create playtime. Engage your family in having fun. Have a "who can make the funniest face" contest or tell jokes and funny stories. Throw a pajama party. Play favorite board games. Rent a funny video. Sing songs together. Make

"Cynthia, have you seen my bobby pins?"

an unscheduled trip for an ice cream cone. Once a month, have a weird breakfast day. Call a surprise party to celebrate your cat's birthday. Have your children tuck *you* in.

Enter your child's world. Join kids wherever they hap-pen to be and savor close moments with them. Build towers with your preschooler, play Barbies with your pre-teen, and listen to music with your teen. All the time, pay rapt atten-tion. Join your kids. Follow their flow. When you cross the threshold into a child's world, you'll feel unexpected warmth and love that wouldn't otherwise surface.

Cultivate touch. Closeness abides where loving touch abides. In your family, learn how to "reach out and touch someone." As you pass by, extend a hug, a light pat, or a shoulder squeeze. Warmly embrace young children sitting on your lap and hold children's hands while walking together. When teens are open and relaxed, tousle their hair or hug them.

Continually encourage your children to reciprocate touch. Tell them, "I love hugs." Institute the notion that "everyone needs eight hugs a day" (or pick your own hug quota) and encourage generous giving and collecting.

In any loving form, touch yields potent emotional dividends. Nothing, in fact, gives us greater assurance of worth and lovability than someone we love affectionately touching us. Loving touch also soothes pain and softens life's blows, communicating where words can't: "You're safe." "I'm sorry." "You're lovable." "You're not alone." Loving touch further conveys a sense of being loved enough and safe enough that others will openly express their feelings. In fact, ongoing

"OK, Billy, your father would love to listen to you play."

"Did you get directions to the next rest room?"

loving touch heightens goodwill and facilitates problem resolution. You can work out almost any conflict with someone
you can hug. And, when you touch with love, you touch the
human soul—your own and others.

Encourage humor. Cultivate your family's funny bone.
Family humor can make you laugh hard and feel deeply with
those you love. Humor strengthens bonds, diffuses volatile situations, heals wounded feelings, and keeps contact harmo-
nious and open. Humor is also a potent means of influencing
kids and creates a delightful synergy that builds unity.

Recognizing the value of humor, some families create a
lore of stories about family life that instantly triggers laugh-
ter and fond memories. All someone has to say is, "Do you
remember when . . ." One family, for example, delights in
telling about their camping trip to Yellowstone Park and how
Mom slept in the car because she was afraid of bears; and
how Dad woke up everybody yelling that there was a bear
in the tent; and how the bear turned out to be Mom, who
was freezing and had quietly crept into the tent to search for
a blanket; and how Dad probably scared Mom a lot worse
than any bear would have.

Humor power can be used to say "no." For most parents,
saying "no" is serious business, and a "no" moment is a

"Wash the dishes? I thought you said watch the dishes!"

potential source of conflict. Parents, however, can often soften their "nos" with a touch of humor. One mother, for example, sometimes sings her "nos"—"no, no, no, no, no"— firmly but lightheartedly.

Using humor to prevent or dissolve conflicts has far-reaching benefits: children then learn to use humor to lighten their own relationships. In one home, for example, when a child makes a mistake and a parent gets cross, the child may

"We have a wonderful day planned for you, dear. And as soon as you make breakfast we'll get started."

remind the parent: "Remember the time when Mom tried to wire the car and it started on fire?" The reminder of that disaster—now a family joke—usually tempers parental response.

Tie family together. To tie or weave your family together, reminisce with them about your parents or grandparents and your childhood experiences. Look at family photos, scrapbooks, and journals, or put together a family tree. Collect and preserve stories about ancestors and give children personal heirlooms to treasure. Bring out your own childhood pictures, tell happy childhood stories, and share memories of your courtship and marriage.

"Allowance time? Okay, here's a dollar for you and 59¢ for your sister."

Keep a family record. Keeping a family record can also strengthen family ties. Take frequent photos and keep a loaded camera nearby. Record important family events via audio- or videotapes and keep a yearly journal of special events and achievements. Review these every New Year's Day.

Establish family traditions. Traditions slow down the rush and chaos of daily life and create familiar, predictable events around which a family can center. Traditions also knit a family together, extending a sense of belonging and of "place" in the universe.

The ways in which families can put together traditions are endless. All it takes is a patchwork of family events pieced together with love and, presto—you have the beginning of an enduring tradition! For starters, consider such potential traditions as Sunday night waffles, a standing Friday night pizza date, a Fourth of July barbecue, or a New Year's Day brunch.

A "birthday table" tradition is sure to be popular. Before the birthday celebration, with the "birthday child" conspicuously absent, together assemble a decorated table complete with birthday wrappings, balloons, streamers, presents, and cake. Later, around the table, celebrate the birthday. If possible, spend the entire day with the birthday child.

Also consider creating a "blue plate" tradition, placing a royal blue plate before family members to celebrate special

"I had a little difference of opinion with another
father in front of the nursery window."

occasions. Tell your children the plate symbolizes goodwill and heartfelt congratulations. It can be used to say: "happy anniversary;" "What a fine accomplishment!" "Good for you;"

"You're special;" "You (won the game) (got a raise) (secured a job) (were promoted) (graduated)."

Such traditions potentially foster bonding across generations: "Your traditions don't disappear when the kids marry," observes the woman whose family created the "blue plate" tradition. "They come back home to participate together in those family events and they begin creating them in their own homes. We, in fact, encourage our 'blue plate' tradition by giving our married children a plate so their families can enjoy the special warm feeling that using the plate generates."

"Which did Eve discover first, the apple or the headache?"

Articulate family values. Invest time, energy, and spirit in your family and define family as coming first. Cultivate the need to safeguard and enhance each other's welfare and happiness. As parents, choose family time over less important activities. Identify other family values such as honesty, responsibility, tolerance, peace, compassion (including compassion for animals and strangers), and model these values.

Nurture spiritual life. Together, reflect on the meaning of life. Read aloud poetry, scriptures, or other inspiring writings. Express your own spiritual values and encourage a loving family atmosphere. Attend religious events together.

A strong family life requires time, energy, and spirit but unqualified investment yields unfathomable returns. As Sir John Bowring observes: "A happy family is but an earlier heaven."

CHAPTER 2

Make Home a Haven

No family has to reside in an embroiled, tension-filled environment. Conflict can cease. Peace and serenity can abide. Home *can* be a haven. So read on for winning strategies:

Opt for peace. Decide that family fighting is an artifact of the past and institute whatever action is necessary to quell family strife. At a family meeting, alert everyone that fighting and other destructive behaviors are off limits. Without finger-pointing, identify strategic ways to eliminate conflict.

"Well, you told them not to play on your precious lawn . . ."

*"Because I don't have time to wash and
take care of my life, that's why!"*

Identify family patterns. Are you and your family
"stuck" in the way you relate to each other? Does it seem that
no matter what the subject or what your intentions you end
up fighting or feeling hurt or angry? If so, members of your
family may be reacting with automatic responses that take
over whenever you're together. In essence, the responses
control the family rather than the family controlling the
responses.

The Allen family, a case in point, remains in constant tur-
moil because members habitually react without thinking
about the consequences of their behavior (or that they have
choices about *how* they behave). As illustrated below, you
may find the following Allen scenario an all-too-familiar
sequence of events:

"Clean your room right now or I'm not going to let you
go to the dance," Janet says to her teenage daughter, Tricia.

"No, that's not fair," Tricia responds. "You didn't make
Rob clean his room before he left a few minutes ago. You're
just picking on me."

Janet looks for reinforcement and turns to her husband:
"Bill, don't let her get away with that. Make her do what I
say," she demands.

The plot thickens. Father, acting as the heavy, physically drags Tricia off to her room to do her work. But Father is frustrated because he doesn't like the way his wife approached his daughter and he doesn't want to get involved. Faced with the choice of fighting with his wife or doing what she says, he defers to her wishes, but he is angry at having to choose between his wife and his daughter.

Mother, Father, and Tricia repeatedly go through this scenario because they draw from a restricted range of behaviors (all ineffective) to work out their problems. All fall victim to the tendency to unknowingly resort to patterned behaviors when responding.

"Dinner still isn't ready yet, huh?"

Interrupt family patterns. Family members separately, and cumulatively, develop a unique blend of both functional and dysfunctional patterns. Functional patterns consist of behaviors that contribute to the well-being of members, such as the ability to listen carefully or to openly show affection. Dysfunctional patterns, consisting of behaviors that wound members and tear a family apart, include such actions as arguing or taking sides.

It may be heartening to know that the choice of even one family member to make positive changes may significantly reduce negative patterns. In the case of the Allens, for example, Janet could decide to approach her daughter with positive requests, appealing with a pleasant tone of voice and perhaps some humor. She could also tell Bill that in the future she wants to work out her problems with Tricia without his help. Since contacts with Tricia have become almost entirely discordant, Janet could begin creating positive moments with her daughter whenever possible.

Bill could ask Janet not to involve him in arguments with their daughter, explaining his difficulty in having to choose between the two. He might also look for positive ways to support Janet in her parenting role, such as giving her feedback about successes she has with Tricia and talking to Tricia privately concerning his wish that she respond positively to her mother.

Tricia, too, could commit to changing her defensive posture and tell her parents what they could do to help her conform to their wishes.

"Oh, no! Harold's run out of 'Mr. Nice Guy' pills!"

*"I want to give you every opportunity to change your ways.
When you don't I'll bop you on the head."*

Change self. Becoming aware of negative patterns is the first step toward replacing them with more positive ones. Watch for the patterns in your family. If you have frequent negative encounters with other family members, it is likely that everyone concerned is perpetuating conflict. Privately try to conceptualize how you and others are behaving. Then ask yourself, "How do I contribute to conflict?"

If you're a family fighter, decide to interrupt your own entrenched positioning. Review the likelihood that you have negative relating styles that add to and promote conflict. If you assassinate the character of others, insult them, or call them names; if you yell or scream; if you are contemptuous, sarcastic or impudent; or if you use profanity or vulgarity, you're an obvious contributor. Equally so, you're a contributor if you aim to control or overpower any family member through intellect, voice volume, body language, threats, or forcefulness.

Write a new script. Potentially, you are a powerful agent for change in your family. Because family fights are patterned, write yourself a new script—when one actor shifts position, others must also. Make a habit of doing the unexpected. Be understanding, try to problem-solve, admit when you're wrong, apologize, tell others what they're doing right or state your wish to stop fighting. In fact, invite an early end to a conflict by expressing love and your interest in repairing the relationship. Use any appropriate positive behavior that will surprise others and cut through detrimental fighting habits.

Seek understanding. Rather than expounding your own view, attempt to see another's perspective. Most people have a preconceived position before an argument ever starts and, as a result, they never seriously consider altering their stands. Therefore, to assure you understand another person's point of view, try paraphrasing that person's view.

*"He was throwing his weight around when someone
pulled the rug out from under him."*

Don't wait for change. If you take responsibility for changing yourself, this doesn't mean others are exempt from needing to change or that problems are your fault. It simply means that you are taking charge and creating favorable life changes rather than waiting for others to make your life easier. (Waiting, in fact, is self-defeating. Others rarely change first.)

Help kids stop fighting. To help kids change their fighting habits, independently explain to them in a quiet and private moment what behaviors you want them to change.

(Tell your kids what behaviors you're trying to change, too!) Then, later draw attention to them when they're cooperating, trying to resolve problems, responding respectfully, treating others in caring ways, or communicating responsibly.

"My husband is very competitive."

Describe their behavior, say thanks, and point out how their actions benefit themselves and others.

Disengage. Quickly disengage from arguments. No one can argue without cooperation. Simply say you don't want to fight. Or say, "I need to withdraw and regroup right now so I don't say or do things I'll later regret." Also say you'll reintroduce the issue (in a few minutes) (in an hour) (tomorrow). Then do it.

Alternately, agree on a code word such as "Peace" or "Truce." Disengage by using that word as a way to temporarily withdraw from a fray.

Also remember that the likelihood of winning an argument with any family member is almost nonexistent; so don't try. Keep out of corners by not making threats you feel compelled to implement; and don't elbow others into corners where they are forced to choose between winning and losing.

Almost invariably, they'll fight to win. No yielding, no giving in, no doing what you want. Period. Then you're stuck. If you exacerbate the conflict, you'll invariably lose. Remember, one of life's most healthy and hearty strategies consists of avoiding battles, not fighting them. A masterly retreat is itself a victory.

Protect children. Spare children the profound devastation of watching you fight. *Constant fighting—terrifying to children—creates incalculable psychological damage.* Agree then with your partner to talk about heavy issues in private. Further agree that if one partner is getting heavy or noisy with a child, the other can quietly step in and take over. If you can't quell fighting, obtain professional help. It's worth it.

"I think there's a power struggle going on here!"

Put people first. Fully commit to the principle that the fragile egos of people are more important than routines or schedules, than broken windows or dented fenders, or than any other momentary thing that goes wrong. Let that firm commitment govern your behavior in any family situation.

Respect privacy. Talk to children individually and privately about problems. Disputes played out before an audience foster damaging political alignments. Further, don't tell outsiders your children's problems—or problems you *have* with them. Children merit the loyalty and privacy characteristic of true friendships. If you need consultation, privately confer with an expert or someone you trust.

"I hate this neighborhood!"

Handle problems you own. Don't slough off problems on your partner and then expect that partner to resolve problems "your way." Independently resolve your own problems with kids.

Establish clear boundaries. Never side with your partner against a child or with one child against another. And never allow children to side with you against your partner or a sibling. Taking sides alienates family members from each other, creating permanent relationship schisms.

Eliminate grimness. Avoid "grim" modes that characterize family interactions. These include any habituated punishment or grounding approaches. Under "kid stress," many parents go grim—that mode where their voices go stern, their bodies rigid, and talk turns to consequences and punishments. Those sights and sounds are forbidding and terrible to children who, if they have many such experiences, find some way of protecting themselves—often through embattlement or emotional withdrawal.

Establish rules. Set up family rules that absolutely ban name-calling, swearing, and other abrasive language or physical violence. Don't wait even thirty seconds to intervene if children violate these rules. Follow the rules yourself.

Intervene. Don't let kids just "fight it out." Nothing is gained by letting children do battle. When children can freely strike out, they learn that hurting others is okay. So when you see escalating anger, step in quickly and simply separate your children, sending them to different parts of the house. The longer you wait to do so, the more bitter the feelings and the more remote the possibility of peace.

If you want to talk to the children involved, speak privately to each one. At a neutral time, clarify with kids that you'll decisively intervene in any hostilities. Emphasize you'll no longer tolerate harsh encounters between family members.

"Spanking or non-spanking?"

Don't spank. Spanking is dangerous to your child's well-being. In the guise of discipline, parents often use spanking to discharge pent-up frustrations and outrage. Ironically, rather than encouraging appropriate behavior, spanking encourages defiance and drives misbehavior underground. Spanking also encourages violence. Children punished through physical means—spanking, jerking, slapping—often imitate such behaviors.

"Your son started teething today."

Contain stress. Children attract adult stress. But instead of using children as verbal punching bags, take a walk or a bath. Hit a pillow. Or talk to someone. Find ways of releasing your stress without stressing out your kids.

Control anger. The starkly uneven power differential between parents and children makes you the heavyweight, so temper your anger. Choose words beforehand that don't wound or bruise fragile spirits. Further, don't express raw anger. Instead, defer to expressing basic feelings underlying anger such as worry, fear, disappointment, love, and concern. Afterwards, rate your exercise in self-restraint. Ask yourself: "If someone else talked to my child like I just did, would I feel all right?" If your answer is yes, you've won a decided victory.

Staying emotionally intact with kids isn't easy. In fact, you'll have to stay on guard. After an intense day of aggravations, it's easy to feel besieged by an exhausted, needy, or unreasonable child. Inadvertently, that child may become a prime target for your spillover anger.

Exit. Sometimes all perspective goes out the window and you need a fallback strategy. When you're losing control, leave the scene—immediately. If your child isn't old enough to understand, make sure that child is in a safe place before you exit. If your child is old enough to understand, say you're blowing your circuits. Say you need some time to put yourself back together; you'll be back when you can talk reasonably about what's happening; say good-bye; and go!

"It's a surprise Mother's Day cake!"

Assess problems. Children often misbehave or have problems. If, despite your best efforts, your child continually behaves in puzzling, distressing, or self-defeating ways, use these questions to assess the seriousness of troubling behavior: How persistent is the behavior? How severe? Is the behavior age-appropriate? Does the behavior interfere with your child's life or yours? Does it hurt others or damage relationships? Is the problem pervasive or isolated? Additionally, has your child's behavior suddenly changed? Is that child depressed? Withdrawn? Agitated? Unpredictable? Unmanageable? Prone to frequent mood swings or temper tantrums? The relative frequency, intensity, severity, and longevity of problem behaviors suggest whether professional help is advised.

Offer compassion. Children aren't just "little people"; they see the world differently than adults. They don't always have the conscience, foresight, or perspective to conform, so extend to them the quality of mercy. Distract them. Put them elsewhere. Tell them what *to do*. Or plan ahead. Outmaneuver kids—don't punish them.

"He's unorthodox, but he's very good."

Model desired behavior. Modeling is a potent way to obtain children's cooperation. If you don't want kids to hit, don't spank. If you want cooperation, be cooperative. And if you want apologies, apologize. To receive reciprocity, model such courtesies as, "Please," "Thank-you," "Excuse me," and "You're welcome." And frequently use the healing words, "I'm sorry," "I was wrong," "Will you forgive me?"

Ask for feedback. Ask of family members: Am I patient? Attentive? Do I listen with my heart? Show my love? Treat you well? Insure your safety and security? What can I do differently? What am I doing *right?*

Use positive touch. Sometimes children don't move on cue, perhaps don't turn off the TV to do a chore or otherwise come when they're called. In such instances, warmly encircle them with your arms, perhaps from behind, and direct them with a soft and loving but firm touch and voice. An occasional kiss on the cheek furthers the message: "I love you, I want you to move, and I'll help you make that move through love, not fear."

Use the "next-time" approach. When children misbehave, clearly label the behavior unacceptable and explain why. Offer suggestions for "next time" behaviors. Describe what you want or what would help in the future. Just as music teachers instruct students regarding which instrumental strings to play, similarly parents must teach children which behavioral strings to play. Only then will parents—as well as teachers—get "quality music."

Develop new lenses. View your children with new lenses that see the quiet, valuable, and elegant behaviors that are always there in miniature. These behaviors all too often go unnoticed and unencouraged because the behavior that usually catches our attention is the kind that makes waves. Sometimes a child's efforts to show caring, to make new friends, to learn new things are so ordinary to adult eyes and so fleeting that they pass us by and are forgotten the next moment.

Examine positive feelings. Recall when your child behaved positively. Were you touched, pleased, proud, or impressed? Or perhaps you were elated, delighted, thrilled, or overjoyed. What engendered your emotions? Did your child learn something new? Did he show affection, compassion, or give generously? When you're stirred by your child's behavior, say so.

Cultivate attributes. As an adult, most likely you want your children to be self-reliant, honest, loyal, trustworthy, industrious, responsible, cooperative, and caring. Affirm these potential attributes as they emerge; for example, when a child *is* telling the truth. Clearly label proactive behaviors consistent with these attributes: "You've worked hard on your homework (all evening) (the past fifteen minutes). That's perseverance."

Regard potential attributes as small, fragile, embryonic seeds breaking ground. Cultivate these seeds, which need protection, nourishment, and warmth, until they become well rooted.

"Here sits little Johnny Birnbaum, the amazing six-year-old who loves carrots, brussels sprouts, broccoli, clean socks, clean underwear, loves to clean his room, loves . . ."

*"This is Jerry, a stand-up comedian, who every night
at nine will bring some humor into our lives."*

Bind family. A powerful alternative to discipline is "positives," the bonding superglue of relationships that delicately shape children's behavior and affirm to kids they're loved and valued. Over time, positives become "child insurance," enhancing the probability children will emulate esteemed values and attributes. Ever so shortly, children will start telling you what *you're* doing right and what they love about you, affirmation that are invaluable gifts and treasures. Finally—interwoven with golden threads of love—positives bind family together, truly making home a haven.

CHAPTER 3

Enhance Marriage

We all get perturbed by the trivial but seemingly monumental actions of spouses (though, says one comedian, it's our own fault. We shop hard and long to find a partner to annoy us the rest of our lives). Nevertheless, most of us could better weather those times when tension builds and we're thinking, "Divorce, never! Murder, maybe!" Below find ways to smooth life's rougher marital encounters:

"If she's not the woman you married, what is she doing here?"

Appreciate the big picture. Couples in enduring marriages appreciate the big picture, viewing their marriages and their partners as invaluable. Such reverence takes eminent precedence over small annoyances, which profoundly pale in relation to marital riches. Illustrating this big picture in *Love and Marriage,* comedian Bill Cosby speaks of his wife and the keen perspective her absence can bring. When Camille is late, Cosby confesses, sometimes he begins "to fantasize with a desperate heart. Has she been kidnapped by gypsies or run away with the circus or simply gone someplace where nobody scratches the back of his head? . . . Why did I ever get angry at her for a silly little thing like keeping me awake till three in the morning with her light on while she read magazines and scattered cracker crumbs on the bed?

"How far apart are the contractions?"

"I'll never get angry at her again, no matter *what* she does," declares Cosby. "I don't care if she wants to use the bed to feed *pigeons*. I want her back, even if she comes a half-hour late, because she's the best thing that ever happened to me."

"Will just toast be all right? I cut myself breaking the eggs open."

Respect differences. Irritated at his wife's preoccupation with a TV soap opera, a husband challenged, "How can you sit there and cry about the made-up troubles of people you've never even met?" "The same way you can jump up and scream when some guy you've never met scores a touchdown," she replied in kind.

In the context of such personal choices, no absolute standard exists—there is no "right" way to dress, eat, walk, make love, allocate time, or even scramble eggs. Despite this, the message "Be like me, think like me, act like me" often underlies partners' pressure tactics to change each other. But partners do have the inalienable right of personal choice. You each have the right to be yourself, who you are, the sum total of your feelings, thoughts, behaviors, tastes, dislikes, opinions, and perceptions. Thus the only viable choice is to invite, not demand, change.

Be selective. Be selective regarding problems you introduce. Think about it this way. The first time an annoyance occurs, it's an accident; the second time, a precedent; the third time, a redundancy. Let the little things go. When you encounter a redundancy, or pattern, perhaps address it. But if your annoyance of choice falls within value or style areas, institute the "Golden Rule for Dealing with Differences": When all else fails, change yourself.

Be an intimate ally. In a marital relationship, two people become intimates in that they live intimately in close quarters, their fortunes and well-being inextricably tied to each other. In that sense, partners can potentially become either habitual Intimate Allies or Intimate Critics. The difference is keen: an Intimate Ally typically expresses love, offers understanding, and extends support. An Intimate Critic does not.

True intimacy, in the strictest sense of the word, requires an emotional and spiritual connection with another and a desire to experience that other's deepest inner self; and to share, in return, one's own. Thus, high marital satisfaction—and low marital stress—is contingent upon partners becoming formidable Intimate Allies. The constant stream of sarcasm, criticism, rebuffs, and putdowns coming from an Intimate Critic precludes the emergence of such intimacy. Intimacy flourishes only when partners join as Intimate Allies, abundantly creating through fresh and encouraging responses, a nurturing marital atmosphere.

*"A seven-year loan: Gee—I doubt if
we'll be married that long."*

Don't fight. To counteract fighting, put your energy into working out your problems, not working *over* your partner. Stop fighting. Fights don't resolve anything. Fights waste time, cause pain, and aren't fun. They shred personalities and create hard-to-heal scars. And no partner has ever gratefully professed, "Hey, thanks for that good fight last night!" Worst of all, partners don't even remember what they fight about, as one woman confesses: "When you get to the end, you forget what happened at the beginning."

Establish a fight-free zone. To counter fighting, agree on fight-free zones—a bedroom, den, garage, or porch—where partners can retreat simply by announcing, "I'm going to my zone." For a fight-free zone to work, both partners must support the wisdom of a circuit breaker and honor the sanctity of any designated zone. Agreeing to the "zone" requires that the other doesn't follow, knock on the door, or shout through the door. Later, the retreating partner is responsible—within an earlier specified time period—to reinitiate possible discussion. However, it must be stressed that most arguments are frivolous, irrelevant, and hazardous, and best not revisited.

"What do you mean, this is my last meal?"

Change locations. Quit dealing with hot topics in the usual battlefields. If arguments over sensitive issues, for instance, typically erupt in the living room or bedroom, try resolving these issues during a walk around the block or during a restaurant dinner.

"OK, you guys have wasted enough of my electricity!"

Circumscribe debate. Limit debate on heated issues to particular specified times on specified days. Then, when spontaneous disagreements occur, relegate them to scheduled discussion times. Circumscribing conflicts to scheduled times ensures ample time to resolve problems and ample time away from having to deal with them. Such action also leaves the relationship wide open to both neutral and positive relating, giving partners breathing room and the potential opportunity to re-experience positive conditions similar to those in courtship.

Institute damage control. "Never go to bed mad. Stay up and fight," advises Phyllis Diller. But it's truly better *not* to stay up and *not* to stay mad. (Sleeping is a stress-reliever—fighting isn't!) So establish a time limit to resolve matters, say, a half hour. When time's up, leave the room and fight behind. If you want the last word, apologize.

Flip coins. When trivial issues can't be resolved, flip a coin to decide who's right.

Institute "odd-even" days. In advance of small crises, agree that on even days, one partner makes the final decision and on odd days, the other partner gets to choose. Use this approach for choosing activities, videos to watch, tasks to accomplish, and so on.

"You know, Howard, all I've ever seen of you at breakfast is your fingertips!"

Regulate airtime. Effective communication is scuttled when one partner typically dominates the airwaves or when both partners speak simultaneously, in essence creating a dual monologue. To counter any such destructive tendency, and to establish an effective and regulated communication tempo, try the following exercise:

As partners, first pick as a topic a simple, low-investment problem and divide a deck of playing cards between yourselves. Take turns making short presentations relative to the problem and then putting a card on the table. When you're the one without a card in hand, remain quiet until your partner finishes speaking. Alternately "spend" your cards until you achieve problem resolution. Repeat this exercise several different times to increase the probability of creating ongoing deliberate and balanced dialogue.

Lighten up. Relieve escalating tension with a bit of well-placed humor. Take, for instance, the classified advertisement that read: "Husband for sale, cheap. Comes complete with hunting and fishing equipment, one pair of jeans, two shirts, books, black Labrador retriever, and fifty pounds of venison. Pretty good guy, but not home much from October to December and April to October. Will consider trade."

After about sixty telephone calls, some of them serious, the wife who placed this ad printed a retraction: "Retraction of husband for sale cheap. Everybody wants the dog, not the husband."

In a simple way, then, humor is a way of moving from "grin and bear it" to "grin and share it."

"That isn't what I meant when I asked for your help."

Allow flunks. Returning home from work, a young man found his bride upset. While pressing his suit, she confessed, she had burned a big hole in his trousers. Consoling her, her husband noted he had another pair of suit pants. That was lucky, she granted, cheering up, because she had used the other suit pants to patch up the hole. This is a pregnant moment. What to do? Blow up? Castigate your partner? Turn her in for a new model? Or overlook the flunk? For best results, choose the latter. Everyone makes mistakes. Think back to *your* last blunder, and then forgive your partner's. Tolerating your partner's mistakes will yield better tolerance of your own.

Overlook flaws. Partners who focus to a fault on each other's flaws perpetually make themselves miserable. In pondering whether to criticize a partner's ostensibly negative actions, a handy rule of thumb is, "Don't."

"It all started when we added a little bathroom."

Declare a statute of limitations. Partners who habitually recycle past grievances never resolve issues. They merely record the other's latest "crimes" in The Archive of Unforgivable Offenses. Then, with updated rap sheets, they randomly indict each other, haranguing each other with a never-ending list of misdeeds over key marital issues: sex, money, communicating, discipline, in-laws, and the like.

"George, please! Not the orange shirt on the green lawn chair!"

In cases like this, both "crime experts" know just how to keep the marital fires smoldering by taking frequent pot-shots: "It's just like you not to want to go to a movie. You don't mind spoiling anything. Why, it's just like on our honeymoon when you . . ."

"I know it's farout, but my husband just disappeared when I pressed the 'delete' key on my computer."

Couples who repeatedly indict each other have imperfect memories that, similar to a video camera's one-way filming, have recorded only the other partner's negative behavior. Neither party can be heard saying, "If you think that's bad, let me tell you all the things *I've* done wrong."

As a remedy, declare a statute of limitations on past crimes. To bring the habit of focusing on the past to a screeching halt, agree together that discussion of crimes, faults, or misdeeds more than twenty-four hours old is off limits. Then, if you're frustrated by recurring behavior, instead of harboring resentments and bringing up incidents weeks or months later, talk about present rather than past incidents.

"It's just until I find his mittens."

Further, when an incident occurs in the present, define how you'd like to resolve it. If you clobber a partner with past actions, you may convey to that partner that his or her behavior is unalterable in the future. Consequently, burdened by past "unforgivable" sins, that partner has no chance to "start fresh." On the other hand, when you ask or invite your partner to meet your *future* needs, you offer that partner a chance to give you an enduring gift.

Establish boundaries. To make this concept operational, imagine a solid, impenetrable boundary encircling you and your partner that preserves the relationship's privacy and integrity. You're both on the inside. Everyone else is on the outside. This critical insider/outsider distinction instills confidence in a protected, safe relationship that then encourages trust, fidelity, loyalty, and security. In turn, these sterling attributes foster a truly satisfying and intimate relationship.

To strengthen and preserve boundaries, implement the following: When you're happy with each other, tell the world. When you're not happy, tell each other—with intent to solve problems. Respect your partner's confidences. Keep details of your intimate and sexual life sacred. Resist forming alliances with outsiders against your partner. If problems arise with outsiders, together resolve those problems, developing strategies to address partner needs and to preserve the relationship's boundaries. Also aim to preserve outsiders' feelings and precious family relationships.

"I've managed to stay on budget, but now I need some money."

"You're right. Maybe we should get a tree."

Go the extra mile. Generously extend favors, kind words, and a helping hand—all gestures that symbolize genuine caring. With loving voice and tone, extend abundant emotional courtesies: "Here, take mine." "Let me reach that." "Can I make you more comfortable?" "Are you warm enough?" "What can I do to help?" Unequivocally convey through bounteous thoughtful actions that your spouse's comfort and welfare are all-important.

"We pause now for two minutes in our newscast to give your wife an opportunity to tell you about her day."

Humor a cranky spouse. If your partner gets cranky, don't get cranky, too. Simply serve the following recipe:

Ingredients:

> 1 adult crab
>
> 1 kettle of "just right" hot water
>
> Liberal amount of light banter
>
> 1 pint of love and affection
>
> Warm towels
>
> Soothing potion of your choice

Directions:

Put crab in hot tub. Provide light banter while crab cools. Add love and affection. Prepare the soothing potion. After soaking for thirty minutes, remove crab from water. Towel dry with warm towels. Serve potion. Crab should lighten up with treatment.

"I see the Johnsons are making up again."

Laugh more. In your courtship and early years of marriage you probably laughed more than you do now. Encourage laughing together by watching a funny movie, reading the comics, or sharing humorous stories. Couples who laugh together are more likely to stay together.

Communicate. Although marital satisfaction and communication are highly related, most couples don't spend nearly enough time talking. Thus, structuring more time together can often enhance or resuscitate a marriage. Author Fritz Ridenour wrote of a husband that during seventeen years of marriage he and his wife had spent more than eight hundred hours talking. And how could he possibly calculate this total? Because, despite major obstacles, every Saturday morning for seventeen years the couple had privately breakfasted together.

"But I liked the old furniture just the way it was . . . paid for!"

Take personal inventory. In any marriage, *being* the perfect partner, not *finding* the perfect partner, is the challenge. Harry P. Dunne writes that in a personal inventory, the most critical question is: "What is it like to be married to me?" In addition to this question ask yourself: What is it like to communicate with me? Make love to me? Work out problems? Eat, sleep, and breathe in my space? Would *I* like to be married to me? And—the most sobering question of all—What would be the outcome if I faced an annual performance review today where either partner, if unsatisfied, could opt out?

"What do you want from me? I've tried everything to show you how much I love you—a new vacuum cleaner, a new washer . . ."

Plan marital upkeep. Relevant questions include: Do you invest sufficient time, energy, and resources in your marriage? Is your marriage amply represented in your planner? Do you periodically review marital health? Does your marriage receive upkeep equal to or better than your house or car?

Protect emotional health. Today, no other malady ravages marriages and families more than mood disorders. And no other malady more insidiously causes stress or promotes divorce. Consider then two vital questions: Are you familiar with symptoms of mood disorders? And, should you have a mood disorder, would you willingly own and address it?

For any sufferer, potential symptoms of a mood disorder include sadness or hopelessness; anxiety or agitation; insomnia or over-sleeping; decreased energy; weight loss or gain; withdrawal and isolation; difficulty focusing, concentrating, and organizing; mood swings; excessive emotion; redundancy of thought; suicidal thoughts; pessimism; numbness;

irritability; and sometimes volatility. In some cases, symptoms may also include unpredictable behavior, impulsiveness, impaired judgment, distortion of information, rage, and cycles of depressive lows alternated with dramatic highs.

Treat mood disorders. In diagnosing their condition, sufferers may believe symptoms are signs of an emotional deficit that must be remedied through sheer willpower. To the contrary, mood disorders are caused by chemical imbalances of the brain. Such imbalances may be situational or genetic in origin and, when genetic, are physical ailments akin to diabetes and high blood pressure.

"We upgraded Mrs. Williams from 'critical' to 'picky'!"

Mood disorders are potentially ulcerative, festering and corrupting relationships like open sores and acting as major contributing factors in abuse and addiction. Because marital and personal stakes are so high, identifying mood disorders is a critical protective measure. Fortunately, when treated—usually with prescription medication and sometimes with therapy—symptoms may be largely neutralized. The bottom line is this: always address a mood disorder if you have one. And don't, under any circumstances, get a divorce in a depression.

Cultivate non-demand touch. Cuddle and snuggle. Hug and hold hands. Nuzzle a convenient neck. Simple, non-demand touch is pretty potent stuff—potent enough that in a 1985 column Ann Landers reported on sixty-five thousand women who had written in to say they preferred being "held close and treated tenderly" to having sex. Yet, non-demand touch is seriously lacking in most marriages.

"I take it the headache you've been suffering from all week is now gone?"

Plan sexual intimacy. Fatigued couples are easily trapped in a downward spiral. She's exhausted and says no. He feels rejected. She becomes defensive. Both get angry. Then recriminations start. As a remedy, become pragmatic. Spontaneity is wonderful, but in today's world couples must be adaptable. To insure satisfying intimacy, reserve several nights a week. By structuring intimacy, goodwill prevails, intimacy increases, and, on "off nights," both partners relax.

In sum, every loving act, every thoughtful gesture, every warm and enduring thought, strengthens a marriage. Simone Signoret said: "Chains do not hold a marriage together. It is threads, hundreds of tiny threads, which sew people together through the years."

CHAPTER 4

Stretch Your Self

Most of us remember an entrenched Archie Bunker from TV's "All in the Family." Suffering from "hardening of the attitudes" and unwilling to listen to input, Archie is a premier stress-generator. Confronted with new ideas, he immediately rejects them, limiting his choices and experiences and restricting his growth. Further, toxic in his effect on others, Archie stymies effective communication, creating a bleak and impenetrable wall between himself and others.

Stuck in his rigidity, Archie is a closed rather than open system. People with such mind-sets are highly intolerant of opposing beliefs, they believe what they know is "true," and they cling desperately to that "truth." In this respect, their attitudes toward life happenings are entirely frozen in time.

"I know it would save his life, but it's a little more than we had intended on spending!"

Conversely, people with open mind-sets quickly absorb and assimilate information. As new information emerges, they consistently examine and revise assumptions, cultivate new ideas, solicit further information, and formulate new hypotheses about the world. Before drawing conclusions, they give fair hearing to all relevant viewpoints. And at times they will willingly live with ambiguity or thoughtful uncertainty. The ability to think fluidly and objectively decreases life stress and increases emotional health. To stretch and flex your mind's muscles, draw from the following strategies:

Opt for growth. Expanding one's view combats the tendency to stagnate—to remain the same. And good reason exists for *not* stagnating: "Loyalty to petrified opinion," reflected Mark Twain, "never yet broke a chain or freed a human soul."

"OK, OK, go play golf with your buddies!"

In every daily event, you opt either for stagnation (defending your views and responding in old, outmoded ways) or for growth (examining your views and responding in innovative ways). Representing a restricted view is the tourist who, when standing before a huge hotel picture window overlooking a beautiful mountain, turned to her husband and complained that she could see the scenery if the big mountain weren't in the way.

"Ralph, can you hear me? If a woman from accounting comes by and says she's a witch, don't laugh!"

Similarly, everyone tends to view life through varying "picture windows," and your interpretation of events always determines how those events affect you. Unlike an open mind-set, a closed mind-set will continue to upset you, creating agitation, chronic pain, or depression. But by broadening your perspectives, you can discover other, more reasonable, explanations—thus controlling your moods and your stress. The more comprehensive your view, the greater your capacity to cope flexibly with a rapidly changing world.

"Don't think of these as restrictions on your lifestyle. Think of them as jobs for the multitude of people who will interpret and enforce them."

Pursue the path of learning. You are most likely to create enduring life pain and misery when you're closed to learning. Paul and Margaret Jordan, authors of *Do I Have to Give up Me to Be Loved by You?*, say that individuals essentially posture themselves to relate either with an *intent to protect* or an *intent to learn.* Those who pursue the path of protection vigorously defend themselves against threat of real or imagined pain, becoming closed, hard, disinterested, cold, and unresponsive. Conversely, those pursuing the path of learning remain vulnerable and open to self-discovery, becoming open, soft, curious, warm, and responsive. Intimate relationships evolve when people, embracing the path of learning, are open and receptive to change.

"All those here for a two o'clock appointment,
please start taking off your clothes . . ."

As such, the path of learning entails utilizing a wide-open lens, deliberately seeking a fresh perspective and questioning your receptivity: Am I rigid and closed to new ideas? Do I resist information counter to my own beliefs? Do I close up and doggedly defend my own views? If you already tend to consistently and consciously monitor your receptivity to information, you're well along the path of learning.

"OK, Sis, eat all the chocolate eclairs because you don't have a
weight problem—but remember, you are the only family
member who has false teeth, fake hair, falsies, fake . . ."

"Look on the bright side, you are alive to hear the bad news."

Examine your measuring standards. Internal measuring standards—idiosyncratic to you—allow you to assess others' behavior, opinions, values, and ideas. However, your standards probably do not measure what is real at all—they reflect only what you know, what you've experienced, what you're comfortable with. When others don't fit your measurements, as perceived through your unique and imperfect lenses, you may find that you label and judge them as inadequate, bad, sick, or sinful.

"Now that scares me!"

In fact, you can impair your own judgments by assuming you know why someone behaves in a certain way. This is where you need to pause, stop making assumptions, and ask. The explanation might surprise you. Consider Dan P. Greyling's account of a woman who was surprised by the explanation for one young man's seemingly arrogant behavior as he sat across from her at an airport restaurant table.

"All those in favor, say 'aye' . . . all those opposed, clean out your desks!"

The woman, who had just purchased a sack of cookies at the airport, sat reading a newspaper and eating her cookies while waiting for her flight. She became aware of something rustling at her table and looked up to see a neatly dressed young man helping himself to her cookies. Reluctant to make a scene, she leaned over and took a cookie herself. The young man in turn took another cookie, until the two had shared all but one cookie. By this time, the woman was fuming. Then the young man took the last cookie, broke it in two, pushed half across to the woman, ate the other half, and left. Later, still angry with the young man, the woman opened her purse to retrieve her boarding ticket and was confronted by her own bag of cookies. She had been eating his.

Negative judgments can be dangerous. Most often, they say more about our own deficiencies than those of others. And sometimes we can get into *big* trouble (complicating our stress) when our judgments come back to haunt us and we have to listen to someone repeat word for word what we shouldn't have said. It appears, as someone once astutely offered, "Nothing is opened by mistake more than the mouth."

Don't rush to judgment. As with the "cookie" woman, at times we're all subject to making harsh and impulsive judgments and then discovering to our shock that our perceptions were inaccurate—if not downright wrong. History is replete with such "wrong judgments," judgments that should a life sentence have been rendered would have deprived the world of consummate talent. Attracted to Hollywood as a young dancer, for instance, Fred Astaire took the usual screen test. The verdict has become part of film history: "Can't act. Slightly bald. Can dance a little."

Countering the propensity to judge others, Flip Wilson taught his children an object lesson. When asked why he had given his children a bulldog, he explained, "So they would see that ugly face and discover all this love behind it—and never take anything at face value in the future."

*"My opinions are based upon intellectual understanding,
experience, and compassion. Yours are just stupid."*

*"Watch out for Nilla. She's looking for the person
who left smudges on her computer monitor."*

Question first impressions. You have probably—and likely more than once—rushed to judgment based on a first impression. Every day, in gleaning bits and pieces of information, we unconsciously "fill in the blanks," making guesses and assumptions upon which we then act. However, such perceptions may be erroneous and based upon inadequate, inaccurate, or unverifiable information. Making quick assumptions, valid or not, can sometimes cause us to become ego-invested in that assumption, solidifying our perception. Then when our judgment is questioned, we may fight for our hasty perspective. This leads to dark-mindedness and combativeness and, heaven forbid, may invite a physical contest.

It's ironic that what most people argue over is almost always a difference in perception and most times certainly not a perception worthy of ensuing hard feelings that could fester for hours or days.

Reserve judgment. Whenever you draw momentary conclusions, stay on alert, ready to revise those conclusions when new information requires it. To increase the probability of reserved judgment and an open mind-set, decline to immediately reject starkly different perspectives. Instead, mentally review those perspectives, even practice defending them. Cultivate a "beginner's mind," a mind receptive to emerging events as though those events were fresh and new.

Increase tolerance. In essence, tolerance is the vision that enables us to see things from another's viewpoint. It is the magnanimity that concedes to others the right to their own opinions and their own peculiarities. Finally, it is the ability to stay cordial, positive, and rational when someone steps on our mental corns.

Eliminate prejudice. Become an impartial witness to your own inner and outer experiencing. To review your own judgments, step back from your mind's constant stream of automatic reactions. Note whether you dichotomize or divide momentary experiences into rigid categories. Ask yourself: Upon what information am I basing my judgments? On proven facts? On personal knowledge? On hearsay? If I queried ten strangers, would they agree with me? Responses will help decipher prejudices and ill-formulated conclusions.

"Uh-oh—battle alert!"

Be aware that you can also prejudice yourself through the words, sentences, and phrases you use to form judgments. For instance, the expressions "an awful attitude," "a rude person," "a dreadful dress," "a disgusting display" all represent global judgments based on opinion, not fact.

You can also prejudice yourself through right/wrong thinking: "I'm always right so you're always wrong." People who are rigid right/wrong thinkers don't grant others the right to be wrong or different. The closer they identify with others, the more they seem troubled by the momentary "wrongness" of others. They may even construe other's refusals to capitulate as a challenge to their integrity. But telling others they're wrong is usually just one way of ruining an otherwise peaceful encounter—nothing more. If you pronounce yourself right and others wrong, your pronouncement doesn't improve your day. It doesn't convince others of their error. It doesn't make people like you more. And it doesn't make you feel good. As a matter of fact, your choice is this: You can be right. Or you can be at peace.

"You have a defeatist attitude, Mr. Hubley. How'd you like to start playing tennis with me twice a week?"

*"Don't do anything foolish—your
insurance premium isn't paid!"*

Temper anger. If even after pensive consideration you still violently disagree with someone's opinion, eliminate that inner violence. People all have their own idiosyncratic and often impenetrable realities. So why unnecessarily agitate yourself? Instead, calmly practice a wide tolerance and serene respect for opinions you can't alter. With exception is the necessity to oppose dogmatic opinions endangering the safety, well-being, or rights of others or their environment.

Even then, craft a deliberate and dignified response—one most likely to temper or negate the threat. President Woodrow Wilson once said: "One cool judgment is worth a thousand hasty councils. The thing to do is to supply light and not heat."

CHAPTER 5

Go with the Flow

In today's accelerating and overwrought world, we face daily, surprise situations that can delay, disappoint, or shock us, even bring out our worst self. An appliance breaks. The kids fight. The toast burns. These are uncertain moments, potentially fueled by hidden avalanches of accumulated stress. But do these little things matter? Perhaps more than we want to admit. But do they matter enough to spoil a moment, an hour, a day? Most often the contemplative answer is no. Many little irritants are maddening but not serious after all—soon irrelevant and forgotten.

"Guess what you'll have to give up?"

"I'm Albert, your waiter, and I'll be ignoring you for the evening."

When little things do rile us, often it is because someone or something has invaded our time or space, interrupted our mental schedules, or challenged our tacit expectations. The affront can come from a total stranger ahead of us in line who whistles, hums, or pops gum. Invading our emotional boundaries, the unwelcome sound jars our mind-set, discombobulates us, and disturbs our well-being.

"Don't do that!"

*"I just asked, 'How was your day, Dear'—
you don't have to bite my head off!"*

At such times, tempers and manners are at issue. The more we approach an annoyance as *temporary* ("this line is short"), *escapable* ("I could leave"), or *probable* ("this *is* a public place"), the better we will cope—and the more control we can exert over surprise stress.

*"You'll find that we're like a family here. We'll
give you your allowance on Friday."*

Anticipate surprise stress. At the very *most,* when surprise stress occurs, apply the preceding perspective. The annoyance *is* short-lived, you *can* leave, and after all, things don't always go right. At the very *least,* forestall a quick flare of anger, grit your teeth, and mutter that this moment is barely worth stressing over. Thus did a commuter on a subway train, ultimately conquering an urge to throttle an unmannered fellow rider.

"If there's a police car outside I'm not home!"

Sprawled out reading a book, this disregarding rider was decisively crowding a fellow passenger. When she politely requested more room, the man refused. At this the observing commuter yelled, "Why don't you sit like a human being?"

"What are you going to do if I don't?" came the belligerent reply.

"Well," retorted the commuter, "for one thing, I'll tell you how that book ends" (Catherine Romano).

Neutralize surprise stress. Individual responses to surprise stress span across a continuum from maximum rigidity and callousness to maximum flexibility and sensitivity. Inherent in fluid responses is "going with the flow"—the knack of managing glitches gracefully with compassion, patience, and tolerance.

*"You're in big trouble, fella—you haven't
filed a tax return since 1979!"*

Those managing surprise stress well anticipate such surprises, deciding beforehand not to personalize or agitate over them. And these people therefore preserve their physical and emotional well-being by not overdosing their hearts on adrenaline. They don't live so tense that they soon become past tense.

"You're in luck if you can handle the stress!"

Be flexible. Admittedly, your greatest irritants in life may be people who won't cooperate or who block your way. Complaining about their "obstinacy" could inordinately preoccupy you, but remaining unaffected is vital to managing difficult people, as one coed demonstrates. Tired of loud conversations outside her dormitory door, she posted a sign: "Whisper—it's sexier."

"I don't like you, Hargrove, but you're
a 'yes-man' and that I like."

Release yourself. In the midst of some life hassle, you've probably stopped dead in your tracks, privately questioning, "Why am I getting worked up?" or, "Wait a minute. What am I doing? This isn't that important." If so, in such instances you took a hundred-and-eighty degree turn in your emotional thrust. By changing your perception of an event and interrupting your push for resolution, you defused your stress. As a consequence, you coped more effectively or mobilized your energies more efficiently. In essence, you released yourself from mounting tension.

"It's customary to give a dollar to each caroler!"

A major component of going with the flow is that of "releasing." When used deliberately, releasing is a method for rapid, on-the-spot de-stressing. In her book, *Releasing,* Patricia Carrington suggests the following:

To learn how to release at will, begin with a simple exercise. Squeeze something soft, such as a tissue, tightly in one hand. Then, as you think the words "Let go," open your hand and drop the tissue, paying attention to what that release of tension feels like. Next practice linking the feeling to a mental formula. Choosing something unimportant, such as an object you'd like rearranged, ask yourself, "Could I let go of wanting to change that for two seconds?"

"I keep thinking we forgot something."

Now practice linking the formula to a number of small frustrations, maybe when you miss the turnoff, or the candy machine eats your money, or when you run out of gas. With each experience of "letting go," of stopping an "overpush" to resolve problems *now,* new options open up and situations become more manageable. Happily, each seemingly trivial thing you release can lighten your total emotional burden.

"Forty million dollars down the tubes and all you can say is 'Murphy's Law'?"

"We've been waiting for so long we decided to redecorate!"

Exercise patience. Do you ever find that you are rushing through life simply to reach the end, ignoring opportunities to exercise patience? To have patience is to practice wisdom; to wait slowly; to be gentle and loving; to let others grow; to proceed at their own pace; to be tender to their feelings and needs; to be compassionate; to treat them with dignity; and to revere their very existence. Finally, to be patient is to open your heart and soul to others, knowing they are your brothers and sisters, created by God. Thus, profound reason exists to be patient and "go with the flow."

"Looks like all the computers are down."

"I didn't realize we were talking so long . . .
Your first payment is due."

Forgive. Akin to patience is forgiveness. Only by releasing yourself from the bondage of an unforgiving stance can you "go with the flow." We have all incurred past hurts, some of us more than others. In any case, you must choose: you can either perpetually occupy yourself with those hurts or you can release them. If you believe people should be punished for the pain they cause you and that you should inflict that punishment, you grant burgeoning life to your grievances. You can nurse those grievances. Or you can forgive.

"We ran out of money right after we built the pulpit."

"Don't concern yourself with it. It's just a little bet I have with one of the other surgeons."

In some instances, understanding paves the way to forgiveness and you may abate your feelings by seeking deeper truths regarding people who have hurt you. Such people may actually be weak, needy, mean, or cruel human beings. If that is the case, simply feel sorrow, as God would, for the tragic loss of human spirit and soul. Your injury has likely been perpetrated by persons who themselves suffered devastating injury.

"And as you can see, it's within a stone's throw of an elementary school."

On the other hand, people who hurt you may be basically good people. Even good people hurt each other. In such instances, consider extending forgiveness. Under reverse circumstances you would wish for the same magnanimity. Finally, ponder whether you inadvertently contributed to problems leading to a particular wrongdoing and are therefore jointly accountable. Such accountability represents all the more reason to extend forgiveness and even to seek forgiveness yourself.

Pastor James searches for the proper words to say "I'm sorry"
for criticizing last week's floral arrangements.

Of note, forgiving doesn't entail allowing others to continue heaping abuse upon you. To protect your self-respect and well-being, you may need to set limits, and sometimes even disengage in relationships.

Sometimes injuries are so personal, so unfair, so brutal they canker the soul. When you have received great injury, pure nobility attends forgiveness, the granting of which must necessarily draw from a greater power. Regardless of the severity of circumstance, in the end you must forgive—not for others' sakes but so you can forgo pain, resume your life, and possibly create a brighter future.

"I hope and pray you're a big tither!"

Allow for mistakes. Allow others to make mistakes without penalty. Frequent blundering accompanies the human condition and thus, no one is exempt. We need to adopt a tempered view of mistakes we all make and, frankly, quit taking ourselves so seriously.

"We missed you this morning."

Remember that there are no perfect 10s. People should not have to be perfect. In fact, by definition, everyone is fallible, simply incapable of being all-seeing and all-knowing. We each have the inalienable right to be wrong and to grow from our mistakes without chastisement. In fact, most of us chastise ourselves so severely for our errors that we don't need the harsh disapproval of self-appointed keepers of the universe.

"Wow! What a game!"

Of our own mistakes, remember that a full and abundant life requires thousands of mistakes. To live up to our creative potential, we *need* to make a goodly number of mistakes every day. People don't love us just for our sterling virtues. They also love us for, or in spite of, our goofs and blunders. Finally, for those who nevertheless are self-conscious about mistakes, remember (tongue in cheek), we're only known for the mistakes we admit.

Use humor. Humor is life's best shock absorber. In managing upsets, humor can encourage and empower you. Humor can also lighten your mood, allowing you to poke fun at things you can't change, as with an anonymous army recruit. Near an army camp, a roadside warning sign read:

"PLEASE DRIVE SLOWLY. DON'T KILL YOUR SOLDIERS." Beneath those words, the recruit had scrawled: "BE A BIG-GAME HUNTER. WAIT FOR AN OFFICER."

Of consummate value, humor can dismantle awkward or confrontational situations. It can also give you "a God's eye view" of yourself. A story is told of William Beebee and President Theodore Roosevelt. Often when visiting at Sagamore Hill, Beebee and President Roosevelt would take evening strolls. Engaging in a customary ritual, one or the other would point to the spiral galaxy of Andromeda—one of a hundred million galaxies—noting that the galaxy is as large as the Milky Way and 750,000 light-years away, with one hundred billion suns, each larger than the Earth's sun. Silence would follow. Finally one would say, "Now I think we are small enough. Let's go to bed."

"You have very entertaining parents, Cynthia."

Reduce expectations. To really "go with the flow" requires graceful management of disappointments. Disappointment attends the human condition. You hope and dream, but inevitably you can't escape disappointment. Within reason, of course, expectations are functional, even vital, providing security and ability to make future plans. But how easily you modify or surrender expectations drastically affects your coping ability.

Not life, but how much you *expect* of life is what generates high stress. You may often agitate yourself when expectations don't materialize. As you know, however, the world doesn't turn on your bidding; only by hanging loose can you avoid such upset.

"Alice, I'm leaving you. Don't hold me back, don't stop me . . . Alice, I'm leaving . . . Alice . . . Alice. . . ."

Go with the flow. Make "going with the flow" a lifetime endeavor. Relax. Spend more time just doing, enjoying, being, and loving and less time evaluating, assessing, analyzing, and interpreting. Essentially, at any one moment, you decide whether to enjoy life. You can choose views that are encouraging, energizing, and enhancing or ones that are discouraging, devaluing, and devastating. You can "go with the flow" or not. Fortunately, the choice *is* yours.

CHAPTER 6

Quit Complaining

Little causes people (and their intimates) more stress than indiscriminate complaining about life and its loads. Yes, it's all right, though not particularly productive, to complain once in a while about something. In fact, at one end of the complaint continuum resides the "once-in-a-very-long-time" complaint about a truly annoying problem. At the other end resides the perpetual "sick-and-tired-of-everything-most-of-the-time" complaint establishing that everything is always awful. We all can afford to move further toward the judicious but just occasional complaint—aiming to make complaining a luxury rather than a lifestyle.

Reduce complaints. Why reduce our complaints? Consider the following: If, heaven forbid, we are among the world's marathon faultfinders, we may reduce fallout on others by deleting our perpetual habit. And, by getting *others* off the best-stressed list, we instantly increase our popularity.

When we complain we may secretly accuse a listener of causing our woes without that listener having a remedy. Or we may verbally and chronically rehearse our sense of injustice with marvelous, years'-old recall. We may even consider ourselves powerless, viewing our problems as something *somebody* (but not us) should fix. We may think, "I've brought this to your attention, told you things aren't right. Because I've done all I can, it's now up to you." Thus we prohibit ourselves from taking initiative or responsibility for our problems. In this respect, we may also deem ourselves innocent and morally perfect because others have "caused" the problem. Therefore, we have the right to be disappointed and incensed that *nobody* (certainly not us) can rectify our problem.

"It's a good thing she's not here to complain about the way they did her hair."

Complaining may fill our conversations with "ain't it awful" talk, bringing our moods down and further confirming our belief that all indeed is hopeless. Or as grievance collectors, we may simply blow smoke about things we can't change, preoccupying ourselves and wasting our own and other's precious time.

Complaining can also draw others into our accusatory behavior, contributing to solidified group or family patterns that in turn support an entire membership's focus on negatives. We may thus participate in "collective depression." We may even begin to make unfounded accusations about others, creating gossip and hearsay about those who can't defend themselves.

*"Good morning, dear. While you were asleep I jotted
down a few things we need to discuss!"*

Finally, by complaining, we may proffer complaints about *ourselves* to others, who can only affirm or deny they are true.

Obviously, by reducing our quotient of complaints we reduce our quotient of stress and misery. So the next time you're out of sorts, don't complain or head for the drugstore. Instead, try these tips brought to you by Alka-Seltzer, Bufferin, Bayer Aspirin, Bromo-Seltzer, Anacin, and Excedrin . . .

"It's the Johnsons—now remember to bite your tongue and count to ten whenever she says I don't mean to complain."

Question your complaint. Ask yourself whether your complaint is valid. Are you objecting to something simply because it's new or different? If your complaint is valid, address it as best you can. Then let go. If your complaint is invalid, remember: "The squeaky wheel doesn't always get the grease. Sometimes it gets replaced."

"We want to sue our plumber."

Pursue alternatives. Problems over which you are upset may seem overwhelming and insurmountable; you may even feel trapped. However, you can always move with or against the stream, exercising choices available through brainstorming. If nothing works, apply for an "Attitude Adjustment"—a mind torque to help complainers stop complaining about conditions they can't affect. You'll learn a lot. One life challenge, in fact, entails acquiring the knack of living gracefully with unsolvable problems.

Relabel. Cultivate the ability to see the promise and upside of every situation. For instance, when a gardener showed his backyard garden to a friend, the friend seemed disappointed that his garden was so small. To this, the gardener responded: "Yes, my garden isn't very large, but it is four thousand miles deep."

"How many times have I told you not to slam that door?"

Realize that life isn't fair. Life *isn't* fair, but many complaints emanate from expecting exchanges to be scrupulously even: One for you, one for me makes everything equal. But in the real world there are *always* inequities, as

Wayne Dyer observes in his book, *Your Erroneous Zones:* "Robins eat worms. That's not fair to the worms. Spiders eat flies. That's not fair to the flies. . . . Cougars kill coyotes. Coyotes kill badgers. Badgers kill mice. . . . Tornadoes, floods, tidal waves are all unfair. It is a mythological concept, this justice 'business.'"

"Who said life is fair?"

A more realistic option exists. In relationships—to balance what you receive against what you get from others—don't apply the concept of *exact equality* to weigh contributions or performance. Instead, apply the concept of *reciprocity,* meaning "measured fairness" or "balance." Without such tempering, "fairness"—a vague concept at best—is most often unachievable. Break then an "exact-equality" habit by declining to gauge relationship performance or contributions in absolutes. Instead, gauge performance in percentages, somewhere between 0 and 100 percent. Utilizing a "percentage framework," aim for rough reciprocity over extended time.

Apply selective neglect. Most little things, particularly

*"If you think it's crowded now, just wait
till the baby-boomers show up."*

those you can't change, simply aren't worth losing breath over. Remind yourself, as one sage advises, "The person who notices the little things has something else he or she ought to be doing."

Selectively share troubles. "Nobody knows the troubles

*"I don't get it. First she gets mad at me for no reason . . . then
she's sorry and wants to make up . . . then she gets mad
again because I don't bring her flowers . . ."*

*"I don't think you'll have any more complaints about
your husband being a pain, Mrs. Jones."*

we've seen—but we keep trying to tell them," says Mignon McLaughlin in reference to our human propensity to indiscriminately burden others with our complaints. But airing grievances indiscriminately doesn't make them better. Rather, we give longer life to what makes us unhappy and shorter life to any popularity.

Be proactive. Rather than creating problems, create

*"I got tired of complaining, so now I just
carry a big book to block my view."*

"Excuse me, but may I go ahead of you?
This is set to go off in eight minutes."

solutions. Decide what would make you whole and happy. Then, whenever you register dissatisfaction, offer remedies that would help, be acceptable, or be appreciated.

Be introspective. When you think about documenting

"I had issues and complaints to take up with you—
but that was before I saw you were such a big guy."

someone else's faults, count to ten—that is, to ten of your own faults.

Be flexible. Fully functioning people rarely complain, particularly about little things like the sky being too cloudy, the weather too cold, the road too rough. Instead, they simply accept things as they find them. "Blessed are the flexible, for they shall not be bent out of shape," says Marilyn Noyes.

Avoid triangular complaining. Triangular complaining differs from standard, dump-directly-on-you complaining. Triangular complaining pulls in others to hear rambling, unsupported accusations, accompanied by vague hearsay evidence. To remedy triangular complaining, direct your complaints to relevant persons, deleting extraneous others from the loop. Most people dislike being company to third-party complaints.

Delete complaints. Finally, when tempted to voice random complaints, adopt the motto, "Don't say anything unless it improves on silence."

CHAPTER 7

Take Responsibility

You've probably felt frustrated when you've heard kids (or even adult kids) say the words: "It's your fault. You made me do it. I'm not to blame." *You* know people are responsible for their actions. You keep telling your children this, but to no avail. Often they just don't feel responsible, and that's that!

Fortunately, children do grow up and can potentially assume increasing responsibility for self. But not all adults

"What do you mean, 'he' did it? . . . There is no 'he' here!"

"How long will I have to feed myself?"

arrive. Actually, most of us haven't completely shed the tendency to blame others when things go wrong. At times, when it comes to assuming full responsibility, we can become little kids in adult bodies. And yet, *not* assuming appropriate responsibility for the totality of our lives adds quantitatively to our stress. When we blame circumstances, we view solutions to problems as residing outside ourselves. And thus by definition we are powerless to affect our lives.

"If you knew you had to replace your divots,
Herbert, why didn't you do it?"

Assume responsibility for actions. Owning our actions and reducing or eliminating stress are inextricably related because, no matter what is stressing us, in the end it is our coping response that counts. By taking responsibility we can position ourselves differently, take charge of problems, and subsequently influence the outcome of situations.

"The seat-belt buzzer scared me!"

Conflicts can serve as reference points. When things go wrong, listen closely to your self-talk. You may be surprised to hear the same themes that make you cringe when they come out of a child's mouth: "It's your fault. You made me do it. I'm not responsible." However, transactions between people are ongoing and mutually reinforcing. In interactions, one person's response impacts the next response, that response affects the one following, and so on. Learn to be responsible for *your* response.

Own your impact. In a budding conflict, difficulties begin when one person denies having influence in the interaction by accusing another person of "starting" a fight. You might say for example, "You did this to me so it's your fault." However, conflict is most often reciprocal or circular in nature: "You did this to me, so I did this to you, so you did this to me, so I did this to you . . ."

"I just want to know what to do with the body."

Applying a reciprocal framework requires the stance that, any time a conflict perseveres, all parties are fully responsible for *all* their own responses. Try this reasoning the next time you clash with someone else. Avoid finger pointing. Own what you did to escalate a problem, apologize for your own negative actions, and let others be responsible for theirs.

"I still can't believe it! The whole jury had PMS!"

Just like kids, some adults tend to forget (or not recognize) the impact of their loud voices or cutting words. They forget the verbal damage they may have inflicted moments or hours earlier—damage now prompting another's defensiveness, retaliation, or withdrawal. And—just like kids—in their heart of hearts, adults often believe they're innocent. They've had no part in creating the problems about which they now bitterly complain. Yet, we don't truly achieve adulthood or maturity until we move from the passive to active voice, until we can say, "I broke it," instead of, "It broke."

Watch your language. Of relevance, the English language is replete with phrases assigning others responsibility for actions or feelings: You hurt me. You make me sick. You make me angry. You make me crazy. You gave me a headache. You depressed me. Yet, *you* are responsible for your feelings or actions. You don't come with a switch that others can flip to make you feel or do anything. (If others had any control, they might flip your switch to the off position or even push your reset button.)

"I wish you'd stop treating me like a little boy and let me play video games like the rest of my friends!"

Use the pronoun "I." Counteract any tendency to assign others responsibility for your actions by amply using the pronoun, "I": I hurt myself, I gave myself my headache, I made myself feel guilty, I made myself feel angry. You'll quantitatively reduce stress when you refuse to let anything become an excuse for becoming inert. Improvement, in fact, begins with "I." The declaration, "I must do something," will always solve more problems than the declaration, "Something must be done."

"It's the cable company and they've located the problem—you haven't paid the bill!"

Shed blame. Assess whether you chronically blame others: "If it weren't for _____, I'd be (happier) (more loving) (more independent) (more successful). Ask yourself whether you hold others responsible for your problems—others who won't "allow" or "let" you resolve present and past problems. Do you blame your parents, children, partner, ex-partner, or boss for your problems? Or do you blame conditions for your unhappiness? Your past? Your job? Your lack of self-confidence? Poor fortune or quirks of fate? A lack of material possessions.

Any time you assign blame elsewhere, you assign control to external sources. Only by focusing inward on your own thoughts, feelings, choices, and possibilities can you assume control. Remember, blaming is a waste of time. It won't change you and it won't change your life. Only opting to take responsibility will.

Be an actor. Finally, of critical importance is assuming the stance of *actor,* not *victim.* Victims run their lives according to the dictates of others, believing they can win others' affection only through pleasing and compliant behavior. They often let themselves be dominated and pushed around, taking cues from others rather than taking self-responsibility and initiative.

Conversely, actors take charge of their lives. Actors take independent action, orchestrate happenings, make their own choices. Actors also realize the futility of trying to win approval of everyone for every act. They do try to please others, but they are unwilling to do so at their own expense.

"I wish there were some way I could repay you . . ."

*"It's not my fault, Mom. It's the left side
of my brain acting up again."*

To put it simply, actors assume *control,* victims don't.
Keep this in mind as you consider basic differences between
victims and actors. Most people fall somewhere along a continuum between these two poles, thus making it important
to identify attitudes that block assumption of appropriate
responsibility:

*"Oh, I had a wonderful childhood until
somebody cut my umbilical cord."*

VICTIM	ACTOR
"I take whatever life deals out. I am powerless to make changes."	"I can control many circumstances in my life. I am an initiator."
"I have no choices or options."	"I create or find choices and options for myself."
"Others are in charge of me. I must ask permission of them and do what they say."	"I am in charge of myself. I trust my own judgment and will determine what is best for myself."
"Other people are in charge of my moods; they make me angry, depress me, disappoint me, hurt me."	"I create my own moods. I am in charge of the way I react to the behavior of others and events they create. When I am hurt, angry, depressed, or disappointed, I create these moods in myself."
"I must please others in order to feel adequate."	"Pleasing others has nothing to do with my worth. I am an intrinsically worthy human being. Others own the problem if they ultimately disapprove of my behavior or choices."
"I wait for others to (notice me) (meet my needs) (make me happy), but they usually disappoint me."	"When I need others, I reach out to them. I ask for what I want and allow others to give to me on their own terms."
"I can't survive without someone who is (smarter) (stronger) (bigger) by my side. If such a person should leave, I will be lost and I will be nothing."	"I am a survivor. Even if I choose to love and live with others, I *can* stand alone. I *can* take care of myself."
"I can't make mistakes because other people will think I'm (dumb) (incompetent) (a failure)."	"As a fallible human being, I'm entitled to make mistakes and I grow by learning from my mistakes. Destructive judgments of others aren't relevant."

"I had a little trouble convincing Fred, but we're here!"

In sum, unlike a victim, an actor is empowered. And, in assuming an actor stance, you can potentially increase control over your life. So why not? If you don't control your life, someone else will.

"All I said was, 'I think your opinions are hilarious'!"

CHAPTER 8

Avoid Emotional Collisions

You've probably ridden in a bumper car—the kind you can find at any amusement park. And you knew that, even if you tried to take that ride without hitting or being hit by another car, you would undoubtedly still collide with other vehicles. Life is a lot like riding bumper cars when it comes to relating to people. You probably go through each day trying to avoid emotional collisions but, despite your best efforts, you still end up in some crashes or emotional fender-benders.

"Uh-oh."

"What do you mean you beat the stress by driving blindfolded?"

Perhaps the emotional collision is a shock. Where there may have been good feelings, now there is hurt and anger, maybe even retaliation. Both of you may strike out or shut down and pull away. The relationship may end up in a wreck—sadly, sometimes permanently totaled. Because collisions, inherent in the human condition, can't be avoided, reduce stress by minimizing their damaging effects through assuming the following stances:

"I work in a pretty rough neighborhood."

"OK, OK, for heaven's sake, I accept your apology!"

Recognize that everyone is preoccupied. First, recognize that everyone you know, including yourself, is simply trying to survive. People are usually looking inward, not outward, preoccupied with their own pain and pressures, rushing around trying to manage life's normal complications or new glitches that keep piling up on the existing heap. Inwardly focused, other drivers are *not* paying close and consistent attention to you and your bumper car. Their blinders inhibit their ability to understand your problems and to view you in perspective. At times, these other drivers do look outward—locate you, notice your feelings, see your needs. But most often they're paying attention to what's going on inside, simply trying to cope, to deal with problems, and to keep their own bumper cars on the road.

Define collisions as accidents. Because people are preoccupied with life, collisions are usually accidents. Most people have good intentions. Just like you, they don't really want a collision or the accompanying pain of any crash. So give them the benefit of the doubt and concentrate on ways to repair the rift. It doesn't matter who starts the problem. Who *ends* the problem does matter.

"I said, 'I come from a long line of shouters!'"

Temper your response. Even if the other person *did* bump into you—*did* actually cause the collision—you choose your response. You can rant and rave, point fingers, or run your bumper car into the other person. Or you can gracefully accept an apology, explore the reasons for the collision, and otherwise decline to accelerate the problem. You can also remind yourself that a true confrontation won't occur unless you counterattack.

"Watch it! This one can't handle stress!"

"Wrong color again, Mr. Kuppmeyer?"

Cut slack. Keep in mind that most people don't communicate effectively. Unknown to themselves, their habitual and self-defeating responses cause defensiveness and bring out the worst in others. And when poor communicators do collide, they usually don't express hurt directly. Instead, they make loud, angry grating noises that cover over their hurt and repel other persons. Thus, to reduce damage fallout, help clean up the accident scene by searching out what caused all the commotion. You might empathize: "I can see your pain. Tell me what you're feeling."

"Before we discuss your request for a salary increase, do you promise not to cry?"

Own your actions. Take responsibility for your own communications. Maybe you aided collision conditions by yelling or screaming, by attacking, or even by glaring, eye-rolling, or door-slamming. Pay attention to other people's reactions. If others withdraw, become defensive, or counter-attack, check your responses—they may be abrasive. Embrace feedback and stand ready to overhaul your response style. Take out collision insurance by making a serious commitment not to wound others.

"After the accident they just started talking about each other's problems."

Exercise damage control. Finally, exercise damage control by letting other people remain angry all by themselves. Listen to them, help them with their problems with you, but refuse to take on their moods. As writer Sherry Suib Cohen suggests, be like the driver who, with his wife, was waiting for an elderly woman to cross the intersection. As the light turned red, the driver behind the couple angrily began honking his horn. In response, the first driver turned off the ignition, got out of his car, and walked back to the second driver. "Here," he said, handing the other driver his keys. "You run her over. I don't have the heart."

CHAPTER 9

Curb Anger in Traffic

Sometimes the littlest things in life are the hardest to take. "You can sit on a mountain more comfortably than a tack," observes one unknown author.

When it comes to driving, most of us would have to agree. Sometimes just a little thing can set people off—the car up ahead crawling along, the one that tailgates or cuts in too close, the light that won't stay green.

"They come from my fits of rage on the road!"

Now, these nerve-racked drivers aren't your "Mr. (or Mrs.) Bad Guys." No, they're the people who wave at their neighbors, who pride themselves in doing good deeds, who are quick to congratulate fellow employees upon a promotion. They're sensitive, they're well-mannered, and they care about other people—until they get behind a wheel. Then those they treat with utmost civility in person become, in their larger worlds, the anonymous others upon whom they inflict their anger and sometimes rage.

"The computer also provides excuses if you're caught speeding."

*"For heaven's sake, George, do you have to
bring your rage home with you?"*

Why the metamorphosis? Because, largely, the anger
these drivers are venting has little to do with road events, but
rather with accumulated stress looking for a home. The automobile becomes a safe, enclosed space where destructive
emotions are discharged seemingly without penalty or pay-
back. But ultimately raging does exact a hefty price.

"I'll do the talking, you do the fighting!"

"Where's the minicam?

When your anger takes over, you're not in control and your judgment is impaired. You're not driving a car—you're aiming it, endangering yourself and others. Raging in automobiles pollutes the airwaves of passengers. Laws protect people from second-hand smoke. Similarly, laws could usefully protect people from verbal smoke. Finally, raging entraps passengers, rendering them hostage to unrelenting anger, a formidable offence toward the human spirit.

"Yoohoo! May we borrow your bathroom?"

"It adds a personal touch to my road madness."

So how do you curb highway anger, put on the brakes, find the off-ramp, and avoid "my fault" insurance? Consider these possibilities:

Exercise. Release accumulated tension through regular exercise. Deep breathing, meditation, or jogging can relax muscles and resolve anger's physical components.

"Oh, the horns don't work—but the other drivers don't know that."

"It is infectious, isn't it!"

Plan ahead. Schedule adequate time for trips. When driving long hours, periodically pull off the highway and stop for dinner, a stroll, or a nap.

Stay calm. Practice being laid back in traffic. Pay attention to the scenery, weather changes, or listen to soothing music. Sing songs. Wave to drivers. Smile. If you start upsetting the cosmic balance, think, "How can I lighten my mood and even laugh at myself?"

So now when you cut somebody off they'll
think of you as a 'lovable idiot'?"

"There you go—blame the man . . . blame the man . . ."

Anchor yourself. Anchoring, a simple mental trick, helps you become your own observer. Use red lights to review your road performance. Or anchor yourself to markers along familiar routes, such as billboards or certain intersections. At these anchor sites instigate positive private speech. Tell yourself, for instance, "I want to be a peaceful person." Use soothing catchphrases as emotional balm: "Firm but calm" or "This too shall pass."

Stay intact. Recognize that you're encountering real human beings with real feelings, problems, and stresses. Treat them as you would friends or family, Sunday manners intact. If other drivers rant and rave or use poor judgment, don't go ballistic. If you do, you're the loser—certainly of your dignity and presence. Remember that other drivers are not likely to notice your emotional antics, but if they *do* they'll just think you're an idiot or an airbag.

Drive friendly. Adopt a calm, noncompetitive attitude. Keep your manners. Turn the other fender. Stay within radarscope. If your engine does overheat, offer a silent apology. If you assume gracious road etiquette and pleasantly yield to other drivers, they often reciprocate. A cardinal rule of the road, in fact, is that courtesy begets courtesy.

Save lives. Finally, drive as if your safety and security, even your survival, were at issue—they are. Superhighways can make bad manners fatal, and you—not your automobile—could be recalled by its maker.

CHAPTER 10

Control Temper Tantrums

Some people don't just get angry. They have adult temper tantrums, wild ferocious moments where they let their anger fly—along with the paperweight and perhaps the nearest dish or hairbrush. And they scream, strike out, and say unforgivable and unforgettable things.

Not many adults survive stressed lives without an occasional temper tantrum. But when tantrums are frequent, they severely damage people and relationships. Of relevance, it's natural to get angry. Anger is a physiological state of readiness preparing us to protect against threat. Adults, however, commonly excuse tantrums by saying they can't control themselves, a convenient but inaccurate rationale.

"But all I said was, 'If I was making this pie. . . .'!"

*"You just can't go around turning off
everyone's cell phone, Mr. Tucker!"*

Adults do have choices and they *can* prevent angry outbursts and thus reduce stress levels. Because anger is a
choice, there is self-help, including anger-management strategies. Note, however, that certain serious mood disorders can
generate frequent instantaneous and uncontrollable rages
that absolutely require professional help. When mood disorders prevail or are suspect, those who frequently rage *must*
obtain medical and emotional aid. To fail to do so is to psy-
chologically decimate and destroy intimate others.

*"I'd like you to meet my wife, our three kids,
and my anger management team."*

"We don't let him out until he has
complete control of himself."

Recognize Problematic Anger. Five signals bespeak problematic anger: (1) anger bouts are too frequent; (2) they are too intense; (3) they last too long; (4) they promote aggression; and (5) they are disruptive. Problematic anger usually involves frequent rages, which are akin to burning a cathedral to fry an egg. Rage itself is almost never justified, even when a potential rager concludes that another person has knowingly, intentionally, and unnecessarily acted in a hostile and hurtful manner. Simply put, raging isn't wise, dignified, productive, or safe.

"I just knew he'd explode when he saw the telephone bill!"

"I always wondered what my wife would do if I took a shower without removing her pantyhose from the curtain rod."

Fortunately, help is available. Below find simple techniques to decrease anger and increase coping skills:

Monitor physical signals. Start noting physiological signals that warn of mounting anger: Your stomach tightens. Your muscles flex. Your heart beats faster. You breathe more rapidly. Your neck and forehead get hot. You're ready to strike. Now what? The answer: Take opposing action. You *can't* explode until your body achieves physiological arousal, so derail that arousal. Try one or more of the following:

1. Talk more slowly.

2. Whisper.

3. Breathe longer and more deeply and tell yourself repeatedly to relax.

4. Change body position: If you're standing, sit down. If you're sitting down, lean back.

5. Keep hands at your sides or in your pocket.

6. Get a drink of water—literally cool yourself down.

7. Take a brisk walk around the block.

8. Punch a pillow.

"Your mother's philosophy is quite simple:
if she can't see you, you can't bug her!"

Use code words. When you feel anger flaring, default to words such as *think, slow down,* or *keep calm*. Rehearse and repeat code words out loud when eruptions seem eminent and privately ask sobering questions: In the end, do I want to be embarrassed, apologetic, or sick at heart? Or do I want to reconcile, be understood, or be closer? How can I achieve these aims?

"Rough day at the office, dear?"

"You'll have to stop blowing your stack, Zimmers!"

Keep a tally. Spend a week counting anger responses. Use a golf counter or transfer pennies from one pocket to another. Do this predictably, and your anger will lessen. Self-monitoring is a potent means of altering behavior.

Keep a daily anger diary. Record angry outbursts and conduct an anger autopsy to discover anger triggers. Interrupt highly patterned behavioral sequences that fuel outbursts.

*"All I remember was saying 'I ain't gonna
take that from you, buddy'!"*

"Old habits are hard to break, eh, Harris?"

Identify self-talk. Record hot thoughts you use to aggravate yourself and feed your fury. Heated self-statements inflame anger: "Who does he think he is?" "He can't do this to me." "I'm going to show him." Labeling other people ("You jerk") or their actions ("That was rude!") constitutes a form of hot thoughts. To modify agitating self-talk, immediately flag red-hot thoughts and buy time by excusing yourself. Get calm, clear, and centered. Ask yourself: Why make a verbal splat? Remember, an ounce of keeping your mouth shut sure beats a ton of trouble.

"He broke it trying to open the tamper-proof packaging of an aspirin bottle!"

"I've never heard of 'software rage' before."

Think cool. Practice exchanging hot thoughts for cool thoughts by dousing hot thoughts with a verbal ice bucket. Tell yourself, for example, "Stay cool. Just take deep breaths. That's right. I *can* cope. This feels better." Also think cool thoughts sympathetic to another's position: "I can tell she's hurt." "He doesn't understand." "They're stressed out."

"I just love this game!"

Picture yourself boiling mad. Most of us never envision ourselves as closed, hard, defensive, and angry. Is this the way you want to be perceived? And what do you want others to conclude when you're boiling mad?

Identify stress conductors. Determine whether vulnerable others are stress conductors. Too often, those most dear to us become innocent targets of accumulated anger and stress. Children, powerless to fight back, or partners, unlikely to walk away, are among the most likely candidates.

Be patient. Finally, to creatively halt anger, adopt fortune cookie advice surviving the centuries: "If you are patient in a moment of anger, you will escape a hundred days of sorrow."

"It's still not ready?"

CHAPTER 11

Diffuse Criticism

Not infrequently, we bump into people who are critical of us. And no matter how they deliver their feedback, whether cushioned by kind words or labeled as "constructive," criticism can pierce our most carefully arranged defenses, evoking feelings of shame, inadequacy, or humiliation. Extreme, unpredictable, or undue criticism can potentially hurt and agitate us, rendering a walloping verbal blow.

"If it makes you feel any better, I liked the joke."

*"Just agreeing with him isn't enough—you have
to agree with him with a straight face."*

Nobody likes criticism, but we're all potential targets of
momentary ire or arbitrary evaluation. The challenge is to
analyze criticism rather than absorb it. To decrease vulnera-
bility to criticism and increase invulnerability to stress,
counter life's verbal jabs and stabs with these strategies:

*"You are the only person I have ever treated
who has cut herself on her own words."*

"I hate it when he finds mistakes in our work!"

Deem criticism subjective. In human relating, criticism originates from one person's ideas about what another person should do to be deemed adequate by the first person. Criticism that conveys the message, "I'm uncomfortable, so you change," addresses a sender's issues, not a receiver's, and thus the sender's criticism will tend to be self-oriented and highly biased.

"I hope there are no hard feelings about my comments."

"Thanks for the surprise party, dear!"

Shore up. When criticized, will you diminish your self-worth? Hopefully not. Your actions, *and someone's criticism of those actions,* are vastly different issues. One person's opinion is simply that—just one opinion. Independently assess the situation, trust your judgment, and keep your self-esteem intact. Remember, any worthy opinion will not attack your character or your worth.

"We are honest with each other. That's the problem!"

"I'm sorry, Mr. Ferguson, but it is a group insurance policy!"

Categorize criticism. View criticism as amorphous and sometimes noisy information conveying what someone *doesn't want* from you. How you proceed depends partially on whether you deem the criticism *valid, invalid, or questionable.* When criticism is *valid,* you'll usually know— you've heard similar criticism before. If so, open to the inherent message of familiar criticism and consider making changes.

"Well, you said I was spending too much time on my looks."

If criticism is *invalid,* state, "We have a right to disagree." Simply separate the sender's opinions from your own and then go merrily on your way.

If information is *questionable,* seek more information. Criticism is often vague, crafted in sweeping generalities, with the words *always* and *never* as regular fare. To clarify message and intent, non-defensively inquire of the sender, "What do you want? How will this help you? Me? Our relationship?"

*"I think he's dead. He hasn't complained
about my weight all week."*

To reiterate, if criticism is valid, address it. If criticism is invalid, ignore it. If criticism is questionable, examine it. Realize, however, that even valid criticism is relevant only to growth—not worth. As fallible human beings, we are ever subject to growth and entitled to make errors in the service of that growth. Thus our errors have everything to do with our growth but nothing to do with our worth. As an invaluable human being (deemed so by our Creator himself), our intrinsic worth, divinely assured, is not at issue.

Consider the source. Does the sender have your welfare at heart? Is the sender reliable and trustworthy? As a caution, never allow someone who feeds on degrading others to crush or devastate you. That's akin, when you have a choice, to saying to someone with a ball and a bat, "Here I am. Hit me."

"The way I see it, punctuation just slows everything down."

Delay your response. When under fire, postpone action and reply until you've assessed the criticism. By deliberately tailoring a response (or non-response), you act, not react.

Don't defend. In relationships, two people often settle into solidified "attack-defend" positions that come into play almost every time they communicate. Obviously, declining the attack position is vital, but so is declining the defend position. Defending only invites more elaborate criticism, aimed at progressively tangential issues. If you defend, you'll feel scuttled every time.

Quell criticism. With chronic criticizers, simply and emphatically assert, "No more criticism!" Repeat this message, and *only* this message, three, five, or even ten times. Use a firm emphatic tone of voice, assertive posture, and sustained eye contact to punctuate your "broken record" message: you're through tolerating incessant disparaging remarks.

"Say what you want about me, Carl—I still can't hear you!"

As you emphatically tell the criticizer, "No more," that person may attack you, change the subject, or otherwise respond in familiar, irrelevant ways. However, stick with your message and don't—*don't*—respond to a criticizer's tangential messages, no matter how tempting. Repeatedly make your point, then withdraw. The next time the criticizer criticizes you, repeat your message several more times. Only by employing the same strategy *each time* criticism occurs will the criticism end.

"You say I'm a jerk . . . can I get back to you on that?"

"Please don't say you want to 'criticize' our love life. . . .
It's more romantic if you say 'critique'."

Lean into criticism. To discourage a criticizer, try sim-ply leaning into or agreeing with particular criticism, a tactic that neutralizes the criticizer's power:

> Criticizer: Aren't you about fifteen pounds
>   overweight?"
> You: "Yes. Actually, probably closer to twenty.
>   Awful, isn't it?"
> Or,
> Criticizer: "You're dumb."
> You: "I know. I'm stupid, too."

Leaning into criticism is an effective way to do life. You'll suffer less and enjoy life more. When criticism becomes annoying, envision digging an imaginary hole with your foot. Drop in irritating criticism, smooth over the hole, and emo-tionally release yourself.

Defuse criticism. Sometimes criticism simply comes out of the blue. When you're shocked and grasping for a response, say, "I couldn't possibly fail to disagree with you less." That ought to stop people dead in their tracks. And you might whimsically entertain the observation, "Maybe what this country needs is more and better mouth traps."

*"I've entered your criticisms of my work into my laptop.
I'll match them with my actions, chart them out,
give you a performance analysis, and generate
a spreadsheet. Shall I charge it to overtime?"*

In defusing criticism, Will Durant's story of Buddha is relevant. "When a simpleton abused him, Buddha listened in silence; but when the man had finished, Buddha asked him: 'Son, if a man declined to accept a present made to him, to whom would it belong?' The man answered: 'To him who offered it.' 'My son,' said Buddha, 'I decline to accept your abuse and request you to keep it for yourself.'"

CHAPTER 12

Reduce Troubles

We have but to pick up a paper or turn on the TV to hear of horrific events occurring throughout the world—events that should clearly drive home our good fortune. But life's little annoyances—a routine interrupted, a meeting missed, a promise not kept—can diminish our perspective. Suddenly, we're agitating over something minor, our larger view obscured, our sense of fortune abated. However, only by keeping our little troubles in perspective can we reduce stress and increase contentment. To keep such perspective, consider instituting the following strategies:

"A whole Bible and you made all the n's backwards?"

*"The last thing I remember was directing
my feet to the sunny side of the street."*

Appreciate small troubles. We often forget that little annoyances are life's "luxury problems," problems that pale in contrast to the daily survival issues of Third World inhabitants. We also forget that we can easily recover from small troubles. Most often we aren't facing serious losses, and *large* trouble looms elsewhere—trouble that is thankfully not ours.

"If it isn't one thing, it's another."

*"We've located your luggage, but I'm afraid
it's just a teensy bit radioactive."*

Put troubles in perspective. Essential to reducing life
stress is putting small troubles in perspective. Most small
troubles are annoying and inconvenient but not critical.
Offering a sense of proportion, Donald Hall reflects, "The
sight of a gravestone, weighty not only in its granite, allows
us perspective on problems as pressing as burnt toast, taxes
and headcolds." To sort out the big troubles from the small,
physician Keith Hooker advises: "Ask yourself whether your

*"Of the three possible routes for the new freeway, the one
that will displace the maximum number of people and
cause the greatest inconvenience is Route C, which
we now recommend for your approval!"*

"That's one of the unfortunate side effects of the medicine."

problem is the equivalent of a lump in your gravy, a lump in your throat, or a lump in your breast."

Plan on small troubles. Troubles are universal, and we might as well accept that we have troubles as long as we live. Therefore it's wise to accept trouble and bear it without complaining. No one can escape the predictable glitches of this world: investing in projects that prove useless, doing work that somebody else undoes, performing well only to watch someone else get all the credit, fixing something until it breaks, misplacing our "get out of jail free" card when we need it.

"I moved the house today."

Grow with troubles. Rather than expecting fewer troubles, our only healthy recourse is to cope better with them. George Washington Carver, for example, was someone who had learned to cope stoically with toubles. Having lost his life savings in an Alabama bank crash and told he was seventy thousand dollars poorer, he mildly responded, "I guess somebody found a use for it. I was not using it myself."

"Just when I thought I'd finally gotten my life under control, my teenage son passed his driving test!"

Troubles are a necessity, subtly insisting on growth and serving as the vale-maker of character. Indeed, by encountering and overcoming troubles, we acquire wisdom and temper spirit and soul. Although we may not welcome trouble, embracing the trouble we do have teaches fortitude and endurance, enhancing our capacity to cope. And, of course, increased coping capacity and growing confidence significantly lowers stress.

"The dog started shedding today."

Remember that troubles are relative. Increased endurance occurs with recognition that we define "troubles" within our own cultural context. A notice posted at a lodge in a Kenyan game reserve read: "Please do not leave your shoes outside the door to be cleaned, as the hyenas will eat them."

Realizing that cultural messages are relevant but not "true" may increase perspective, especially when you imagine how absurd your troubles might appear in another culture. Just imagine, for instance, someone in a third world country stressing over delays, traffic jams, computer crashes, lost Palm Pilots, or fitting into last summer's bathing suit.

*"You would think you could change one simple light
bulb without making a big production out of it."*

Forget your troubles. If you want to forget all your
troubles, just wear tight shoes. It's amazing how a simple
little discomfort can lend perspective to otherwise discon-
certing troubles. Novelist Jassamyn West describes an unfortunate experience in which, during a college composition
class, she was assigned to write a paper on living life deeply.
Her unconventional ideas apparently shocked her instructor,
who copied West's theme onto the blackboard and for a full
class period discussed the writer's moral and intellectual
shortcomings.

*"Dear, we have an itsy-bitsy, teensie-weensie, problem
with the car and our bank account."*

"Oops—too late!"

West was so humiliated she decided to kill herself and planned a dramatic demise. Starting out the next morning, dressed in white and properly shrouded, West fully prepared to drown herself. But discovering the reservoir gate shut, she left to have breakfast before making a second attempt. She enjoyed breakfast so much she forgot to remember her troubles and ultimately decided to live on.

"Amazing! First time I've ever heard a biological clock ticking."

"Do you want to put that on your credit card?"

Stay out of trouble. A good recipe for staying out of trouble is to spend 60 percent of your time attending to your own business and 40 percent leaving other people's business alone.

Keep your troubles. From another perspective, we might ask, "With whom would I trade troubles?" At least we're acquainted with our own troubles. We also know

"Try to visualize it after $60,000 worth of repairs."

*"I'm not only having a bad hair day,
but now I'm having a bad you day!"*

enough about ourselves to anticipate future troubles. We're at home with our troubles, and the familiar almost always appears safer than the unfamiliar. So don't envy other people's troubles—even if those "others" seemingly have a pretty cushy life. Vicki Bendfelt reflects: "My grandmother always had a prescription for people who liked to worry. She'd say, 'If everybody put his troubles in the middle of the room, you'd run like the dickens to get yours back because theirs would be worse than yours.'"

*"I'm afraid you're going to have to stop
burning the candle at one end."*

Carry your troubles. When you expect others to bail you out of troubles, you get in trouble. Others often don't help, don't help enough, or don't help well enough. And thus you frustrate yourself and shift responsibility elsewhere when only you can resolve your own troubles.

Check your attitude. Attitude dictates how much you *do* suffer over your troubles. You may not be able to change your past or the chance behaviors of others, but you can play the one card you possess: your attitude.

"Please help us. We went into debt buying software on how to live a stress-free life."

Reframe your troubles. Cultivate the art of reframing or redefining troubles so they are no longer problematic. Simply call your troubles "experiences" and remember that every experience helps you grow. Life's lessons are abundant, just waiting to happen, and experience is that wonderful vehicle that provides them. Experience is a handy thing, helping you learn how to predict your next mistake. From experience, you can also recognize a mistake every time you repeat it and know when to cringe. And one thing about experience: if you don't have any, you're likely to get a lot.

Even in the midst of frustrations and disappointments, if you think about experiences and troubles as being really,

really, good for you, you can sustain a sense of contentment. Life is hard, and you do have to work at it. But if you can face difficulties or trying tasks with peace in your hearts, you can know something of happiness. In this respect, author William Lyon Phelps taught: "If happiness truly consisted in physical ease and freedom from care, then the happiest individual would be neither a man nor a woman; it would be, I think, an American cow."

"Oh, hi, dear. You can come in if you leave your troubles on the doorstep."

Realize that troubles pass. Some days you wake up on the wrong side of the world and you know it's a bad day when: You discover your waterbed has broken and then you remember you don't have a waterbed. You turn on the morning news to a display of emergency routes out of the city. The bird singing outside your bedroom window is a buzzard. You open your mail and find an audit notice from the IRS. You get a phone message from your son saying, "It wasn't my fault." Your brilliant brainstorm turns out to be a brain trickle. You leave work early to avoid the evening rush and get stuck in traffic. You think things can't get worse and then you see flashing red and blue lights in your rearview mirror. You hunt for aspirin and realize you're out of aspirin . . . and Alka-Seltzer . . . and Tums. You decide to go to bed but realize your only set of bed sheets is still in the washer. Finally, you look at the calendar and discover today was the longest day of the year. And you can believe it.

With respect to such troubles, remind yourself, "Things could always get worse." But more important, troubles pass. Admittedly, sometimes life does get tough. You will have bad days; but on other days the sun will seemingly shine on everything you do and angels will guide your path.

Predictably, most troubles pale with a good night's sleep and a fresh start tomorrow. And tomorrow, yesterday's bad day will seem just that—one bad day. Advises Lewis Thomas, "The great secret known to internists, but still hidden from the general public, is that most things get better by themselves. Most things, in fact, are better by morning."

"It's just not my day . . ."

CHAPTER 13

Challenge Worries

Any habit of anticipating "troubles" and worrying over them quantitatively adds to stress. Everyone does some worrying, of course, and a little worry may not be bad. Anticipating problems can motivate you to perform at a higher level or help you plan ways of coping. But worrying should not take a significant toll. It shouldn't cost you sleep, distract from work, or lower your self-esteem. If it does, you may be a chronic worrier. Consider the following ways to decrease worry and increase well-being.

"Oh-oh, looks like Mrs. Culver can't sleep again."

*". . . Partly sunny except for these darn
worry clouds coming your way."*

Identify worry patterns. For worriers, the flow of wor-
risome thoughts can be relentless and seemingly uncontrollable. Fretting intrudes upon awareness, saps productivity,
and dampens life's pleasure. In fact, the word *worry* is
derived from the old German word *wurgen,* meaning "to
choke or strangle." By extension, the term eventually came
to denote "mental strangulation," and then the condition of
being harassed with anxiety or care.

*"I didn't want to take the time to run a lot of tests on you.
I thought I'd save you a lot of money by waiting
for the autopsy results."*

"Well, am I contagious or not?"

One characteristic of chronic worriers is that they generate a series of catastrophic hypothetical scenarios and then try to envision their implications. These scenarios take them far afield from the original worry, their mind-spinning activities preventing them from solving the problem. Psychologist Thomas Borkovec explains that worry patterns often follow circular paths: "That important job at work, what if I can't meet the deadline? I might not get the promotion. I might get fired. How can we afford to live if I get fired? How will I make the payments on the car? That car already needs transmission work. If the car is in the garage very long, how am I going to get the kids to school? . . . I've got to save money for the kids' education. I've got to meet that deadline at work."

Eliminate excess worry. The biggest problem for worriers is not that they worry too much, but that they worry ineffectively. Most often, when excessive worry is a simple habit, the trick is putting worry to work and cutting out any excesses. (In exceptional instances, worry is symptomatic of a genetic mood disorder, representing a symptom of repetitive thinking. If you have always worried excessively and, in addition, manifest such other enduring symptoms as depression, difficulty focusing and concentrating, sleep disturbance, and pronounced irritability or anger, consider seeking professional advice.)

Rate your "worry stress." To break a simple worrying habit, first rate your "worry stress" on a scale of one to one hundred. Then rate how stressed you would be if the events you're worried about actually did occur. Most worriers report that they're more stressed by anticipation of events than by events themselves. Next, consider whether your worrying is worth the work. Can you change the future by worrying in the present? Finally, ask yourself how many of your worries have actually ever materialized.

Sort out worries. Divide your worries into three categories: (1) those you can realistically do something about (exercising more); (2) those you can't (the weather); and (3) those over which you have limited control (wrinkles). Tackle worries you can act on. Shed worries you can't control. Exercise any limited power to change events.

*"I'm sure you'll like the apartment,
there are no cockroaches in it."*

Worry is of value when it forces you into action. Therefore, when change is possible, craft a step-by-step action plan and decide how soon to worry. Also minimize worries by sharing them with someone close. As one young child confided to her mother, "It's too much work to worry alone."

*"I'll have her home early, Mr. Farns.
I don't want to violate my parole!"*

*"I'd like to ask you all to keep extra quiet
today—this is the captain's first solo."*

Make a worry list. Gather up worries and write them
down on a worry list. Then date and file the list, retrieve the
list the following week and note items you're still worried
about. Review your list in another week, after that in another
month. You may even want to save the list to review next
year. What will you find? Probably that worrying didn't help,
or even that it was a serious waste of energy. Most worries
will disappear within a few days. In a week, month, or year,
they'll all likely be gone, and unless you check the list you
saved you won't even remember worrying about them.

*"Yes, you're covered for disasters . . . If you were invaded by
aliens from the planet Gexpytl, Zyoqtl, or Plxustz . . . "*

*"Good morning, Mr. Charles. Time we
talked about home security alarms."*

Pick a worry period. Finally, set aside thirty minutes
every day and worry only during this period. Worry in the
same place at the same time and, above all, worry for the full
thirty minutes. In a worry session, you may find that particular worries simply aren't significant. Or your worries will fade
simply because you're concentrating on them. Ultimately,
you may pinpoint and resolve real problems.

*"I figured the best way to handle stress
is to get on top of my problem!"*

CHAPTER 14

Unclutter Your Life

There are in this world inveterate "clutter collectors," people who save things of less than infinite value and then have to live with all they save. And, as gift buyers, gadgeteers, and shoppers, most of us inadvertently become clutter-bugs. And clutter not only clutters our lives, it also clutters our minds. So, if crammed cabinets, stuffed closets, and paper chaos are driving you bonkers, read on for clutter-control strategies.

"Yahoo! The junk woman cometh!"

*"You're going to make some unlucky
girl a wonderful first husband!"*

Recognize stealth of clutter. Simply by default, clutter grows in almost every niche of our lives, clutter we don't need, don't use, don't remember we have, and through indecisiveness will probably store forever. This clutter becomes a form of visual noise, beckoning to us, indicting us, calling us slugs. We agonize over our disorganization, making ourselves feel bad, lowering our self-worth, sapping our energy, and creating our own guilt festivals. All because we've never decided *not* to be clutter-collectors.

*"It's for her own protection. Whatever
she touches she has to buy."*

*"I made a list of everything we own . . . there were a few
items missing, so I went out and bought them."*

Worse, most things we buy are of transitory usefulness,
soon eligible for the category of clutter. Finally, almost everything we own, whether we care for it properly or not, is ultimately subject to deterioration and uselessness, ultimately
destined to Good Will, the junkyard, or to that big Recycle
Bin in the sky.

"This junk mail is getting out of hand!"

"Sold to the lady whose husband just fainted!"

Value time over things. Alarmingly, clutter robs you of time. Remember that everything you own represents things to clean, organize, shuffle, sort through, pick up, rearrange, catalogue, store, protect, insure, and then perhaps ultimately discard. And every new item, every little trinket you collect, becomes a potential enemy to simplicity and organization.

"OK, I separated the stuff to shred from the stuff to file . . .
but for the life of me I don't remember which is which."

Of vital import, you have only so many hours and minutes on this earth. You might ask yourself: Do I really want to fritter away my very limited earth time, a servant to what I own?

Seek clutter relief. Clutter collects through myriad tiny sub-conscious decisions (or indecisions). Each time you add "things" to your drawers or closets, your piles or nooks, you potentially heighten your accumulation of permanent "stuff." Your neglected projects, stacks of paper, burgeoning closets, and overwhelmed shelves represent unfinished business and can weigh heavily on your mind.

"But I didn't know there was a clutter police!"

In tidying up the clutter problem, ask yourself, Why do I diligently collect so many things when things collect so easily by themselves?

Make decision-rules. As a first line of defense against chaos, you can develop little decision-rules to protect yourself. You can decide to "file, not pile." Allocate a place for every "thing" and once a day put these "things" in their places. Fend off the relentless influx of new things. Quit buying so much "stuff." Buy space organizers. Put substantial wastebaskets in every room. Forever commit yourself to clean, organize, and throw away clutter as you go along.

Manage paper glut. Of greatest priority in de-cluttering is managing the paper glut that can daily muddle your mind. If possible, equip your home with a paper-control center, complete with desk, filing cabinet, bookshelves, and counter space. Both at home and work, establish an inclusive immediate action file for every paper that crosses your desk or haunts your mailbox. Label folders by task: To Call, To Write, To Hold, To File, To Pay, To Read. Open mail next to your action file. Keep a waste-paper basket nearby and chuck junk mail without opening it. Every day, sort mail into the system and skim the To Read and To Hold files.

"I, for one, am glad you only go around once. I'd hate to come back and have to clean up this mess!"

Create a filing system. In a central home location, set up a simple permanent filing system. Use colorful organizing files to make the task of filing less tedious. Establish files for every category of information you need to reference: receipts, warranties, titles, deeds, insurance, will, and so on. In one place, file every paper even remotely relevant to tax preparation. Every day clear your home or office workspace. Put new papers in order and out of sight.

"George, it's UPS, again."

Clear your workspace. If your workspace is a disaster, first square up paper piles and boxes and start ordering your clutter. Sort random items by category into seven or eight labeled stationery boxes. Prioritize and store the boxes, later systematically organizing their contents. As you move through your paper mountain, tackle tasks that yield the quickest results. Every target checked off boosts morale and heightens resolve. As free, clean space becomes a reality, savor your victories.

". . . And this is the room where I put all those things I buy on a whim."

"So, tell me, Gloria, when you talk to yourself are you talking about where you're going to put all your stuff?"

Resist convenience items. Consider how much you clutter your life by obtaining timesaving or specialized conveniences that you then must inconveniently maintain. Yes, you can undoubtedly use basic items—a mixer, blender, juicer, rice steamer, multi-use pot, waffle iron, or even a Belgian waffle maker. Not too bad for a start.

But what if you add an Italian tomato press, an asparagus pot, a stock blender, a rotary cheese grate, and in-sink

"Wait, dear—don't sell the playpen!"

colander, a kitchen torch, a ceramic compost container, a commercial cream whipper, a produce washer-dryer, and, finally, a sausage maker? These are only kitchen items, but in today's technological world we could multiply this accumulation elsewhere a hundred fold. For instance, have you thought about buying a CD player for your shower? Or spray-on hair? The list goes on ad infinitum.

By itself, of course, one convenience doesn't pose a clutter problem, but an accumulation of conveniences does. When poised to buy still another convenience item, ask yourself this: "Am I buying a true convenience or simply adding to a burgeoning convenience collection?" Your answer may be telling.

*"After spending eighty thousand dollars, son,
we thought it was the least you could do."*

Prioritize clutter targets. Say good-bye to daunting clutter by developing a list and prioritizing your targets of attack. Work for short periods at a time, pursuing maybe one box, drawer, or closet a day. Arrange pots and pans, put tools into a toolbox. Throw away your stack of magazines, those old concert programs, the years-old recipes you always meant to try. Progressively removing these unsettling annoyances will yield surprising comfort and visual peace of mind.

Organize a junk raid. And now, my Fellow Clutterers,

"For heaven's sake, Carol, let them go, let them go!"

take comfort. There is a professional about who knows how to clear real junk: Gladys Allen, an organizational expert. Allen, who calls her approach, "Remedial Home Management for the Organizationally Impaired," understands that homes are stuffed with "unsolicited" or "unloved items." By conducting a junk raid, advises Allen, you can lose two hundred pounds in one day. So here's how to play "hard-ball" with junk:

"I warned you—if you get in the way you get put away!"

First, buy some huge plastic bags and make sure they're black because if you can't see what's inside, you won't have second thoughts about keeping items that make it to the bag.

Second, put papers you feel are important in a paper saver box. Keep moving! Don't stop during your raid to read old love letters, poems, or to go through magazines.

Third, start with one closet or drawer. Experience victory in conquering an area that, when you're through, contains only items you care about. *Don't,* however, try to commit sudden vengeance and in one mad attack wipe out fourteen years of clutter. You'll only end up in a depressing pile of rubble.

"I swear this is heaven!"

Fourth, designate an emotional withdrawal box. Though you *know* you don't need certain items, you may feel that giving them up is sacrilege. If you're too attached, if your emotions are too overwhelming, don't fight them. Put these items in your box, put a lid on the box, and put a date on the box. In six months, call a worthy organization to collect the box. Put the box out on the porch, run into the house, turn up the stereo, and wait for the moment to be over. Remember, it's almost guaranteed you won't miss the items.

Finally, use "Keeper Questions" to help you lose your two hundred pounds: Do I need it? Do I use it? Do I like it? Will something else do the job? And most essential: Do I have room for it in my life *and* in my mind?

CHAPTER 15

Become Stress Hardy

No matter what your lifestyle, there's no escaping stress. You can, however, always weather it better. To become increasingly stress hardy (and to lead a fiber-enriched and fortified life), choose from the strategies below:

Simplify. Reducing stress requires living in more direct, unpretentious, and unencumbered ways. In today's frenetic world, you incur distractions, clutter, and pretense that can heavily encumber your life. When you remove these impediments, you experience tranquility that emanates only when mind and spirit wed in the context of simple living.

"Stressed? I'm not stressed!"

"I still say we should have gone to Hawaii with our luggage!"

Maintain things. Cut out constant aggravation. If your alarm clock, shoelaces, windshield wipers, appliances—whatever—are broken or broken down, fix them or get new ones. Systematically and in a timely manner, maintain what you own.

"Hey, wait!"

*"I finally fixed that leaky faucet all by myself—but
I screwed up a few other things along the way."*

Plan ahead. Fill up the gas tank at the one-quarter
mark, maintain a well-stocked "emergency shelf" of home
staples, replenish stamps early.

Reduce tasks. Some tasks are essential and others can
be abbreviated or eliminated. On your weekly calendar, trim
away the least important. Making tasks a matter of judgment
and choice reduces stress.

"No doubt about it. You've caught a computer virus."

"On the plus side, your bulletproof vest worked very well."

Review housework. Never in recorded history has anyone finished housework, so make housework a job, not your life. Can you dust or vacuum less often or in less time? Try setting a timer for thirty minutes, de-limiting certain task times. For that matter, involve family members in timed, half-hour pick-up projects.

Meet stress head-on. Eliminate daily patterns that trigger predictable stress. Plan ahead to avert repetition of surprising new stressors. Anticipating stress and gearing up your coping skills creates a sense of control.

"Well, we finally got rid of your brother and his family."

Accomplish something. We all thrive on tangibles—the things that please our senses. So daily do something with your hands, no matter how small. Pleasure at accomplishment overrides stress.

"See? He's apathetic and spiritless—maybe
we should show him his bill."

Take a break. When you feel overwhelmed or your performance is flagging, take a break and do something instantly gratifying. If you work long hours at a word processor or computer, periodically stand up and walk around to relax muscles and rev up circulation.

Take a catnap. For fifteen minutes, close your eyes and retreat from stress. Taking a short nap lowers your blood pressure, reduces your heart rate, and recharges mind and body.

Get aerobic. The world's most effective de-stressor: any sustained aerobic activity that relaxes muscles and causes release of endorphins. To generate these "feel-good" chemicals at work, schedule a midday workout or take a brisk walk. At home, weed the flowerbed or sweep the porch. Do *anything* active and you'll feel better.

Create a cozy environment. A discordant office environment takes a heavy toll on morale. Pay attention to comfort, noise, lighting, and privacy. Check the height of your desk and chair. Make your workstation more comfortable.

Trade a desk lamp for bright overhead lights. Decorate with flowers and family pictures—reminders that work isn't everything.

Be time-smart. Avoid peak times for stores, banks, and post offices. Make early-morning appointments with your doctor and dentist. Grocery shop late evenings, especially during holidays. Catch early evening showings of popular movies or go to restaurants early. In essence, live "off-peak" to avoid time-wasters.

"I'm sorry, Webster, but you were twenty minutes late, so we sold your desk."

Wait gracefully. Waiting can be viewed as a glitch or as a gift, a welcome pause from usual life demands. Use waiting time, don't fuss over it. Make waits almost pleasant with a "to-do" project or interesting paperback.

Create flexible time. Allow yourself flexibility. Rather than scheduling every minute of every day, leave open time blocks for emergencies or downshifting. Also allow extra time to accomplish something or arrive somewhere. Then when you're delayed, you'll feel less stressed.

Keep a journal. A journal can anchor you to your life and helps you organize events and make them more manageable.

"Who installed your car phone for you?"

Say no. Saying no can mean saying yes to yourself. When making larger commitments, head off an automatic yes by deferring a decision. Say you'll have to think about it for a few days. If you say no to things that don't matter much, you can say yes to things that matter most.

"That's not what the doctor meant by 'watch your weight'!"

"I have a feeling this diet is going to work!"

Move on. Have you been party to long, drawn-out, one-way conversations when you wanted or needed to move on? In lieu of listening impatiently, interrupt politely but firmly. Simply say (with as many repetitions as needed), "I'm sorry. I have to go now."

"This is George's first week without a cigarette, caffeine, sugar, or salt!"

"We never should have given him a beeper."

Decrease phone time. A phone, especially a cellular, may become all consuming, interrupting meals, delaying departures, and diminishing relationships. To reduce stress, check your tendency to jump every time a bell rings. Make answering a phone a choice, not an obligation, and exercise your freedom *not* to communicate. In your day-timer or Palm Pilot, schedule generous "off-call" time blocks for personal and family activity. When phone solicitors call, with dispatch ask that your name be deleted from their lists.

Nourish yourself. Put yourself on your daily "to-do" list and don't default on yourself. Engage in a just-for-you activity such as painting, reading, playing tennis, walking, even watching an interesting movie. Invest in yourself by developing skills or enjoyable hobbies. Insure that your life includes fun, lighthearted diversions, and regenerative activities. Balance your life and nurture your whole self.

Garden. Gardening offers exercise as well as earthly meditation. Growing and tilling gardens can be soothing to one's soul. Plus, stress and gardening are incompatible. Just try feeling pressured or hurried while you're admiring your first ripe tomato.

*"I'm watching my cholesterol—so I'm
only laying two eggs a week!"*

Limit caffeine. Too much caffeine *causes* stress, sending your system into overdrive. High intake raises blood pressure, increases muscle tension and agitation, disrupts sleep and digestion, and destroys vital B and C vitamins. Control caffeine effects by limiting your daily intake. Better yet, think health. Choose decaffeinated drinks, juice, or even milk—real brain fodder.

*"That rattle you hear is all those vitamin
pills you take rolling around."*

"We take our 'no smoking' policy very seriously!"

Reduce sugar. A temporary sugar high isn't worth the crash. Sweets make blood sugar soar and then suddenly drop, leaving you cranky, weak, and unfocused. Choose instead high-energy proteins and complex carbohydrates.

"I think our problem is we react to stress in different ways."

"First, I'll need a week off to recover from this exhaustive interview."

If you drink, limit alcohol. Like sugar, alcohol—a depressant—takes you on a high-low emotional roller coaster ride. Creating an artificial, chemically induced state of stress, alcohol causes high levels of tension, anxiety, and lethargy. Moreover, alcohol is hazardous to relationships. Even small amounts can promote anger, withdrawal, and depleted judgment, leaving others vulnerable to "a drinker's downer."

Mind your B's and C's. Stress interferes with absorption of important nutrients such as calcium, the B-complex vitamins and vitamin C, so consider supplements. Calcium, a stress reliever, particularly relaxes muscles.

Eat regularly. If you skip breakfast or lunch, you'll feel edgy. Control stress by instituting a good eating plan, including cereals and grains, fruits and vegetables, dairy products and protein. De-emphasize sugar and fat. Eat three well-balanced meals daily to keep energy high and risk of colds and flu low.

Snack. Eat healthy in-between snacks to moderate blood sugar level. Some best-loved foods can counter the impact of stress on your body. Pasta, low-fat cheese, and that apple a

"My secret to a trouble-free life? Take care of your teeth, don't drive fast and never order anything in a restaurant that gives you gas."

day can help keep you calm and collected when the pressure's on.

Drink water. Nutritionists often recommend eight to ten eight-ounce glasses of water per day. Your body particularly requires this oft-forgotten yet essential nutrient when you're under pressure.

Maintain a regular schedule. Your body needs regularity. Synchronize your internal clock with external events serving as time cues: mealtime, exercise, work activity, rest periods, and—the most powerful cues—light of day and dark of night. Help your internal clock keep you ticking.

Get adequate sleep. To sleep well and to help regulate body rhythm, rise and retire at standard times. Avoid eating late. If you're hungry at bedtime, choose a high-protein snack, perhaps cheese and crackers. Add a glass of warm milk, raising your serotonin level, to induce sleep. Sit in a comfortably hot bath for twenty minutes. Or exercise several hours before bedtime, increasing body temperature, which, as it lowers, causes drowsiness. Chronic lack of sleep erodes health and lowers productivity and stress tolerance. Conversely, adequate sleep adds quality of life and likely years to life expectancy. A good night's sleep is life's most effective stress eraser.

CHAPTER 16

Bargain without Bickering

Picture yourself a member of a board making decisions with other board members. Hopefully, you're listening carefully to others, showing respect for their opinions, and making decisions agreeable to everyone.

Now picture yourself addressing a problem with your spouse or child. Are you attacking problems or people? Are you solving problems or creating them? Are you eliminating stress or generating it? Most people can maintain their manners in board meetings, but forget this gracious posture with family members. Skills that aid problem-resolution in the outer world are gone and forgotten, replaced with grim modes of attack.

"If we find him innocent he'll walk out of here a free man. But if we find him guilty, there'll be media rights, royalties . . ."

*"Harry, if you're ready to see things my way, I'll tell
you where I hid the towels and your clothes."*

Negotiation, however, provides a surefire method for
resolving disputes without battle scars. There's nothing tough
about bargaining without bickering, but you do need guidelines. To their detriment, many couples lack an operative
decision-making model, floundering whenever issues arise.
One partner tugs. The other pulls. Tempers fly. A power
struggle ensues. Someone wins. Someone loses. But ultimately, both are losers.

"To tell you the truth, my wife makes all the decisions."

By learning to negotiate, partners can adopt a guiding framework for smooth relating. Preliminary to contemplating this framework, consider four negotiating positions:

I count, you don't. In this position, partners vie to win by finding fault, blaming, and disagreeing, canceling out any option to negotiate.

You count, I don't. Here partners discount their own needs. They submit, please, placate, agree, apologize, or diminish their influence by responding in these or other non-representative ways.

Neither counts. By default, partners exclude themselves from viable decision-making by being irrelevant, changing the subject, leaving the scene, or otherwise interrupting problem-solving processes. Whatever happens, happens by default. No one takes charge.

Both count. This position, the only growth-producing choice, allows viable negotiating. Only in this prevailing position can couples achieve closeness and intimacy.

"I take it you would like to talk about the thermostat settings?"

Any time partners share close space, they make multitudes of decisions that potentially don't factor in vital needs. Over time, solidified functional or dysfunctional decision-making patterns emerge, dictating how partners habitually relate. For example, when assumed by both partners, the stylized position of "I count, you don't" insures chronic competition and leaves each party perpetually frothing.

"Oh, you'll just love our 'Easy Payments'!"

"This is an audit, Mr. Beemers—not an audition!"

Similarly hazardous is when one partner assumes the "I count, you don't" position and the other partner takes on the "You count, I don't" position. The passive partner may develop growing bitterness and resentment toward the aggressive partner. And much to the aggressive partner's shock, the passive partner may suddenly exit the relationship.

"You want me to do the work of two men when you don't even pay me what one man gets?"

"I know you guys are 'worry warts' and always stressed out—so I thought it would be better if I called the fire department."

In resolutely adopting the guiding philosophy to opt for win-win solutions, partners can neutralize destructive patterns. Essentially, each partner commits, "I will represent *your* needs and assure *you* are satisfied with decisions." Thus each becomes protective of the other's interests.

By adopting the following guidelines, partners can implement a "win-win" approach:

Reserve time. Set standard times to try new problem-solving skills on small problems. Tackle one problem at a time and—*no matter what!*—stick with it. Introducing extraneous subjects confuses issues and short-circuits negotiation.

Dialogue. Only by taking turns can partners truly have a dialogue. Thus, assertive partners with a propensity to monopolize discussions must hold back, allowing less assertive partners latitude to speak. Conversely, passive partners must assertively speak out and represent themselves.

Do the unexpected—be approachable. Say such surprising and stunning things as, "I see your point" or, "I want to understand your position."

Be task-centered. Be task-centered (intent on negotiating) rather than personality-centered (intent on winning).

Use energy to resolve problems, not to establish who *is* the problem. Find common ground. Be hard on problems and soft on people.

Use opinion language. Use language to convey your opinion. Use message lead-ins such as, "From my vantage point . . ." "The way I see it . . ." or, "It's my opinion that . . ."

Identify needs. Reduce problems to their simplest form, that is, to basic human conditions. These conditions include needs, for instance, to feel understood, loved, appreciated, accepted, or counted in.

Begin with needs, not solutions. By identifying needs, you can generate options to address those needs. Entering negotiations already having invested heavily in a particular solution scuttles problem-solving every time.

"Now remember, don't pay manufacturer's suggested retail price!"

Brainstorm. Use "possibility thinking" to generate multiple creative options. At first don't worry about being practical. Have fun. Be imaginative. Propose even silly options. In itself, the ability to brainstorm is a problem-solving skill.

"Your table will be ready in a few minutes."

Don't criticize. Create a "no-risk" negotiating atmosphere by entertaining even the seemingly most ridiculous solution. You can relax because both partners must ultimately, *mutually* agree on solutions. Casually and noncritically entertain ample options before bringing closure.

*"I let him win the arguments—it's easier for him
to take when we still do things my way."*

Rate options. Individually rate options by using a "fitness" scale, where 1 means, "This solution absolutely won't work;" and 10 means, "I'm totally pleased with this solution." Choose the solution when your scores are added together that has the highest numerical rating.

Adopt a winning approach. After practice runs, you'll understand both the philosophy and steps of "win-win" negotiation. You'll resolve problems informally, sometimes on a dead run. You'll retire nagging problems. You'll become advocates, not antagonists. And, the best part, you'll have peace and peace of mind.

CHAPTER 17

Communicate Effectively

Maybe you want your spouse to be affectionate. Or to see your point of view. Or to listen. Or to drop some disagreeable behavior. Or to dress differently. Or to run an errand. Or . . .

You may want a spouse to make changes a dozen times a day simply because those changes suit you or make you feel comfortable. Wanting change is fair. How you go about getting those changes may not be. Through destructive means, partners often pressure their spouses to change. However, relationships improve and partners de-stress dramatically, when they trade control tactics for influence skills, which are skills that invite rather than demand change from a partner. These attainable skills, any of which can create warmth and closeness, are described below.

As you read on, consider whether you use these skills with your partner. (In the communications of troubled couples, these skills are largely absent.) If skills are lacking, you can bring new vitality and satisfaction to your relationship by acquiring fresh communication habits.

Listen. Listening—the "receiving" skill—allows you to understand your spouse. When you're truly listening, you pay absolute attention. You enter a partner's world, trying to understand things from the inside out. You verbally walk with your partner, figuratively holding your partner's hand.

You experience your partner's feelings but do nothing to add to, or change, that partner's perspective. You are not there to judge. You are simply there.

"What happened to your communication skills?"

Anytime you listen carefully to your spouse, you give a gift—a verbal backrub. And you help your partner to clarify elusive thoughts. As you listen, almost magically, a partner will shed hurts, change views, solve problems, grasp larger perspectives. If then you want listening to work its magic, incorporate these tips:

"When I said 'tonight's the night' what I meant was to take out the garbage!"

*"I thought you said that bumper was
good for up to ten miles per hour."*

To reach out to partners, *frequently* listen. Paraphrase responses to reflect the essence of their messages. Use lead-in phrases such as, "It seems to you. . . ." "I sense you're feeling. . . ." or, "As I hear it, you . . ." If you sense feelings, perhaps anger, hurt, disappointment, worry, or resentment, capture those feelings in words ("You're hurt because no one called").

"I said, 'Listen to me'!"

Make a point of listening anytime your partner is wounded or distressed (even if that partner is distressed with you!). Clear your head to simply receive information. Give yourself the strong and certain command, "Now hear this!" Privately commit to understand (but not necessarily agree with) your partner's feelings or point of view. Listen until feelings have dissipated and the *real* problem is evident. Only then explore solutions to the problem. (Well intentioned, most "listeners" are primed to give advice before a distressed person finishes a first sentence.)

"Now why can't you be a little emotional like Shep?"

Use "I" messages. Listening helps you understand others. "I" messages help you understand yourself. With "I" messages—the "sending" skill—you claim ownership of your feelings, thoughts, needs, and wishes:

- *I'm* disappointed we missed the game.
- *I'd* prefer a different approach.
- *I'd* appreciate your fixing the screen.
- *I* feel diminished by your remark.

"I" messages stand in stark contrast to "you" messages, which evaluate, blame or criticize:

- If *you'd* bought tickets we could be at the game.
- *You're* sure dumb doing things that way.
- Why don't *you* ever fix that screen?
- *You're* always negative.

*"You're behind the times as usual, Arthur!
I'm not a nag, I'm a consultant!"*

Whenever your responses put emphasis on another person (you), your inner alarm button needs to go off. "You" messages obscure your deeper feelings and foster another's urge to defend or fight. To eliminate defensiveness and counterattacks, stay with "I" messages.

A stirring of feelings inside can alert you to the need for an "I" message. Silently put negative or positive feelings into your own words: "I'm (hurt) (disappointed) (angry) (sad) (glad) (happy) (excited) (delighted) about. . . ." Also take responsibility for *how* you convey negative feelings. Avoid abrasive voice tones and responses ("I'm disgusted with you!").

"I told you not to put out the welcome mat."

Clarify your feelings through specificity. Instead of saying, "You never help anymore," say "I need help." Further, when you describe heavy feelings ("I felt abandoned at the party"), shift immediately afterwards to a listening stance. Be ready to listen and to understand any discomfort of the other person. Don't respond with another "I" message until you've listened several minutes. Stick with a ratio of five, ten, or even fifteen listening responses to every "I" message. Alternate listening responses and "I" messages until tempers cease, tension wanes, and positive feelings prevail.

"There! That should stop the interruptions."

"Tell me if the light bothers you, dear."

Make requests. When you want something, ask for it. This may sound simple, and it is. Most people, however, don't make requests. Instead, they badger, nag, lecture, and generally just make nuisances of themselves. To shift gears, consider these ways of making effective requests:

"George . . . George . . . Where are you? I promise to yell at you in a nice, positive way . . ."

On the flip side of any complaint is a request. Go for that request. Instead of saying, "Why don't you ever clean up after yourself?" (a complaint), say, "I'd appreciate your cleaning up after yourself" (a request). Keep your request brief and positive. Avoid negative riders that negate viable requests such as, "Thanks for picking up after yourself for a change." Also couch your request in language inviting the other person to respond: "Would you be willing . . . ?" or, "How would you feel about doing . . . ?"

Grant your partner the legitimate right to say no. If that partner is tentative about a request, invite a counter proposal: "Could you help another way?" Or propose another option: "How about considering this . . . ?"

Accentuate positives. When you make requests, be appreciative when they are granted. Always, when you get what you want, tell your spouse you're pleased (if you are) with the change. When you consistently affirm what you *do* like, and what you *did* get, you'll be amazed with the results. For spectacular success, just keep on accentuating those positives. Nothing is better for heart and soul.

"Here are the things I expect from our relationship, dear!"

CHAPTER 18

Relax

Life's a pressure cooker. Before you blow . . . or fizzle . . . put a personal relaxation plan into your daily routine. The goal: To elicit the "relaxation response"—a physiological and restorative state of profound rest. This response, involving muscle relaxation, lowered heart rate and breathing, and "tuning out," can be elicited in many ways. Read on and consider choosing from below several on-point, daily techniques to achieve the relaxation response:

"OK, now tell me about your day!"

"No, no, not that deep of a breath, Mr. Cornwall!"

Breathe deeply. Deep, relaxed breathing is the single most important skill in managing stress, feeding the body vitally needed oxygen for energy and repair. You always require a steady, fresh intake of air. Most of us, however, use our lungs at only one-third capacity and thus don't take in enough oxygen. Instead, we take shallow, rapid breaths from the upper portion of our chests, depriving ourselves of full oxygen supply.

To breathe deeply and correctly, use your diaphragm to pull in air and fill lungs from the bottom up. The diaphragm, a muscle resting at the base of the lungs and floor of the chest, is dome-shaped. As you inhale, the dome drops downward, increasing the size of the chest cavity for the air to rush in. As you exhale, the dome flattens upward, forcing the air out.

While sitting, to gauge how fully you breathe, place one hand on your abdomen just below your rib cage. When you breathe you should feel your abdomen swell outward. Don't force a deep breath, but draw air in gradually, becoming accustomed to oxygen intake that completely fills your lungs. Practice full breathing until it becomes natural. It's worth the effort.

Full breathing, inherent in all relaxation strategies, is paramount to achieving the relaxation response. When you breathe slowly, using your diaphragm, you nourish the body and help cells produce energy. The natural, in-and-out rhythms relax you while the increased oxygen flow instantly increases energy. It's an unbeatable combination.

Check your posture. Stress, many times exacerbated by slouching, often settles in the neck and shoulders. As a preventative measure, try keeping your head, neck and shoulders aligned. Also reduce muscle tension by not cradling a phone between shoulder and ear, or watching TV or reading in bed.

Relax your muscles. As illustrated below, many different de-tensing exercises can offer instant relief to aching muscles:

Shoulder de-tenser. Whenever you notice your shoulder muscles tightening up, relax them by shrugging your shoulders. Inhale deeply and raise both shoulders as high as you can, then exhale fully as you drop them down. Hold each position for five seconds; then return shoulders to relaxed position. Repeat several times. To otherwise reduce shoulder tension, simultaneously roll shoulders back and around and up a number of times.

"Aha! And all this time I thought you came to the toolshed to tinker!"

Neck releaser. To relax neck and shoulders, roll your head clockwise several times, stretching your neck and shoulders. Repeat, going counterclockwise.

Back relaxer. On a carpeted floor or padded surface, lie on your back, bend knees, bring them up to your chest and clasp your hands around them. Gently rock back and forth along the length of your spine. Feel each vertebra being massaged as you rock. Breathe deeply.

Depressurizer. Stand in a doorway and press your palms against the door frame on both sides. For as long as you can, hold your breath and keep increasing the pressure. Feel the warmth rushing to your face, head, and neck. Release. Inhale deeply. Repeat three times.

Feet reliever. While sitting, use your hands to bend and move your toes forward and backward. Then, try doing the same thing with your toes without using your hands. After, lie on your back, raise your legs, and elevate your feet on a chair or against a wall.

"Get your feet off the table—you're not at work!"

Practice deep muscle relaxation. Rather than fighting tension, go with it. Sit or lie down, close your eyes, and take a few deep breaths. Next, alternately tense for five seconds, then relax for thirty seconds the muscles throughout your body: your hands, biceps, face, shoulders, chest, stomach, legs, and feet. Following each muscle tensing, focus on the subsequent feeling of relaxation.

"Better hurry with those reports—she's starting to lapse into her daily daydream."

"Mommy went to her secret place to relax."

Meditate. Meditation's goal is to still thoughts that evoke stress. To meditate, pick a word and silently repeat that word over and over to yourself. If you prefer, whisper the word repeatedly. Concentrate only on the word you are repeating. If other thoughts or distractions occur, simply return your focus to your chosen word. With practice, you can use meditation at will to restore, replenish, and regroup.

"The first thing you've got to do is forget everything your first wife taught you."

"Henry, you've been up there an awfully long time!"

Be mindful. Mindfulness is the ability, through breathing, to achieve increased present awareness. To practice mindfulness, feel the air expand gently on the in-breath and fall on the out-breath. Stay focused on your breathing for the duration of each in-breath and out-breath, riding the waves of that breathing. Momentarily back off "inner busyness" and let your mind drift, embracing your inner experiencing. You can practice mindful breathing while you're walking, making dinner, or just sitting. Spend some time each day simply *being,* not *doing.*

Daydream. Take a refreshing break by kicking back in a chair and letting your mind daydream. All you need is a quiet room. Get comfortable. Then close your eyes, breathe rhythmically from your diaphragm, and blot out distractions. Stay in a state of suspended animation for ten or fifteen minutes.

Visualize. Visualization involves, through imagining, consciously withdrawing from your world for brief periods. With eyes closed, and breathing rhythmically, visualize tension draining out through your feet. Set distracting thoughts adrift, letting them float away like leaves on a stream. Imagine a scene of total beauty and calm: a meadow, an empty beach, a mountaintop. Place yourself in the scene and its quiet mood. Be there completely. Feel the sun, the breeze, the smell of flowers or pine on your face or body. Hear the rustling of leaves, water splashing, or other natural sounds. Briefly stay there, alone in your private unreachable inner space, returning refreshed, focused, ready to move ahead.

"John is adjusting nicely to country living. He has hay fever, poison ivy, and lower back pain."

Use music. Use uplifting lyrics to experience deeper truths. Or listen to soothing instrumental music and let yourself float with the melody. Imagine yourself in a soothing environment and allow the music to relax your muscles. Music can impart positive, affirming, and healthy messages.

Head for the tub. When you're feeling frazzled or craving serenity, take a bath. Add foaming bubble bath or soothing fragrant oils to the water. Spend time in the water with your eyes closed. Experience the sensations: wetness, warmth, tingling.

Breathe fragrance. Breathing in fragrance can be

"I'm worried. All our workaholics called in sick today."

instantly refreshing. Surround yourself in scent. Spray your favorite cologne into the air above your head and savor the scent as the cologne disperses. Or with eyes closed, sit comfortably, relax your body, take deep breaths, and enjoy the fragrance of a freshly cut lemon or an orange or fragrant essence oils.

Get a massage. A centuries-old panacea for tension is massage—a hands-on technique that rubs aches and pains out of sore, overworked muscles. Massage can improve muscle tone, increase circulation, release muscle toxins, and make the skin more supple. And massage, now both affordable and readily available, decreases stress and increases energy.

Give a massage. Given with loving intent and sensitive hands, any massage is bound to please. The only other necessities are oil or lotion, a padded surface, and your spouse, child, or friend. To massage, use pressure, varying for a particular stroke or different parts of the body. Rather than straining your arms and wrists, use your entire body weight to add pressure. Also use rhythm, smooth, consistent, flowing movements, even when stroking vigorously or rapidly.

"Stop rushing it!"

The basic movements of massage fall into four categories: stroking, kneading, friction, and percussion:

Stroking is accomplished by moving the entire surface of the hand over the skin, with palms and fingers slightly cupped in firm, even, long movements. Stroking always moves toward the heart.

Kneading, the manipulation of muscles, involves grasping, rolling, squeezing, and pressing movements. Other kneading movements include lifting muscles between the palms of both hands or with thumb and fingers of one hand. Also directional to the heart, kneading is done slowly with gentle pressure.

Friction involves moving the skin and surface tissues over the bone or other deeper structures. With palms or thumbs in rotary movements, apply friction by using pressure firm and deep enough to move, but not bruise, tissues.

Percussion—always tempered and modulated—includes hacking, alternately striking a muscle with the edge of each hand; pounding, with a half-closed fist; tapping sharply with fingertips; and slapping, using cupped palms and fingers.

With percussion and all other massage movements, elicit consistent partner feedback regarding intensity and pressure of touch.

The different basic movements of massage therapy are easy to learn and progressively master. Couples, incidentally, can invest intensively in a marital relationship by taking a massage therapy class together. Little furthers a marital relationship more than partners' periodically massaging each other with soft, gentle, firm, rhythmic non-demand touch. A relationship is also enhanced when, throughout a day, partners stay in emotional touch through frequent light and loving physical touch.

"But I love you just the way you are!"

Heal thyself. Use your own healing hands to reduce your body's muscular and mental stress. Breathe slowly and deeply as you massage different tension areas. As you inhale, imagine your breath flowing directly to and relaxing the tense places. As you diffuse and exhale through your entire body, release all fatigue, soreness, discomfort, and tension.

*"I need to relax for a while. Would you mind
watching the kids for the next three years?"*

With your hands, you can give yourself body massages in many different ways, including the following:

Face-and-scalp massage. Lying down, give yourself a face-and-scalp massage. First cover your face with your hands and rest in the darkness a moment. Then use your fingertips and thumbs in stroking circular motions beginning at the forehead, sweeping down to the temples, along the top of the jawbone, beneath the cheekbones, and back up the bridge of the nose. Fan out along the scalp with continued pressure and circular motions, pausing at the tender points above the ears and at the base of the scalp, where tense muscles tend to knot up.

Neck-and-shoulders massage. Reach with your fingers up over your shoulders and as far down your back as you can, pressing the fingertips hard on either side of the spine. Squeeze and knead as strongly as you can, moving outward from the spine and upward to the shoulders. Use your right hand to knead the left shoulder, and vice versa. Then, using the right hand for the right side and the left hand for the left side, move hands up along the neck of the base of the scalp.

Foot massage. After a hectic day, take a few minutes to gently massage your feet. Using both hands, massage each foot from toes to heel, then slide hands up the ankle. Fill a basin with warm water and add a few drops of an essential oil with relaxing properties. For ten minutes, relax, give your feet a soothing soak, and delight in the fragrance.

"It's your personal trainer—he doesn't feel like working out today."

Stretch. Tense muscles trap lactic acid, which accumulates in uncomfortable knots in muscles. Stretching helps break up these knots, releasing lactic acid into the bloodstream. Stretching also refreshes, invigorates, and relaxes. And stretches are effective warm-up and cool-down exercises.

You can stretch anywhere and anytime. When you need a break, just stop. Take a deep breath and stretch. You'll be amazed with the results.

Four general pointers:

1. Get those shoes off, substituting slippers or heavy socks if necessary. You'll feel better.

2. Forget bouncing, forcing, straining, and jerking. Stretching should be slow and gentle,
   pleasurable and natural.

3. Before every stretch, inhale deeply and fully,
   expanding your stomach first and then your
   chest. As you move into the stretch, slowly
   exhale all air out of your lungs.

4. Move slowly into each stretch, breathing
   deeply and stopping at the point where you
   feel muscle tightness.

For variety in your stretches, draw from these possibilities:

Body stretch. Raise both arms, stretching toward the ceiling, then bring arms down to the side, hands crossing over
in front of you. Then stretch your right arm upward and over
your head to the left, bending at the waist. Repeat several
times, alternating arms and sides.

Neck stretch: Lean your head toward the right (as if you
were trying to press your ear into your shoulder) and hold
for five seconds. Then lean your head to the left for five seconds. Finally, let your head hang down in front, pressing
your chin to your chest, for another five seconds, repeating
as necessary.

"That's it, woman—can't you just feel those buns burning off . . ."

*"We were rolling our heads around to relax,
and I guess I got carried away."*

Upper back and shoulder stretch. Sitting cross-legged or kneeling, cup fingers behind your head. Using your left hand, gently pull your right arm to the left. Hold twenty to thirty seconds. Repeat stretch, pulling your left arm to the right.

Lower back and shoulder stretch. Kneel down on all fours, with your hands and knees on the floor. Then bend your torso forward and walk your hands way out in front of you, keeping your back and neck in alignment. Feel the stretch in your back, shoulders, and sides.

Hamstring stretch. Sitting, with legs extended in front of you, gently bend your torso down over your legs, keeping your back straight and your neck in alignment. Feel the stretch in the back of your legs and lower back.

Palm press. Sitting cross-legged, press your palms together in front of your body, making heels of hands meet firmly, elbows out to the sides. Hold five seconds, release, and repeat.

Chest opener. Standing or kneeling, close hands behind your back and gently raise your arms as high as comfortably possible, bringing shoulder blades together. Hold twenty to thirty seconds.

Side reach. Extend both arms overhead and slowly reach toward the ceiling, one arm at a time. Now extend your left arm, softly rounded, overhead. Gently lean toward the right. Hold twenty to thirty seconds. Switch arms and repeat stretch to the left.

Knee-to-chest wrap. Lying on your back, bring your knees toward your chest, loosely clasping your arms around your legs, inhale. Exhaling, gently press your thighs to your abdomen. Release and repeat several times.

Inner thigh stretch. Sitting, bring the soles of your feet together and allow your knees to drop open. Gently hold on to feet with hands and pull feet in toward you. Slowly round torso over legs until you feel a gentle stretch in inner thighs.

Back and buttocks stretch. Lie on your back, wrap your arms behind your knees, and gently pull both knees to your chest. If you're comfortable, lift your head toward knees to increase the stretch in the back, shoulders, and neck.

Full-body stretch. Lie comfortably on your back and extend your arms overhead. Push your heels away from your body and reach your arms in the opposite direction. Feel your whole body stretch and lengthen.

"I don't care what they say—I feel better before I come in here!"

CHAPTER 19

Seek Solitude

Much of your health as a human being depends on quiet moments of solitude. Solitude nourishes the spirit, salves the soul, and reduces stress. Solitude introduces you to the riches of your inner interior. And solitude can attune you to a Power greater than yourself, ever assuring that you are never alone. Stress and solitude are mutually exclusive; the absence of one invites the other. Thus, in a frenzied world, we must actively further our own solitude. To do so, draw from the following possibilities:

"Well, you argued for a room with a view!"

Pursue solitude. In today's world, undisturbed solitude is becoming increasingly rare. Ironically, this is often by choice—"I can be alone only if my mission is constructive." But being alone simply for refurbishment and repair seems, to many people, to be discreditable, somewhere between selfish and irresponsible. Thus, such people deny themselves solitude. And they may even disparage or disrupt others' chosen solitude.

"Turn back, Harold—I forgot to set the VCR!"

But the repair, maintenance, and enhancement of body and soul depend upon our capacity to be alone. And, interestingly, being alone can actually constitute a luxury, another's presence potentially detracting from, rather than enhancing, an experience. In fact, sometimes a worse fate than being alone is wishing you were.

Distinguish loneliness from aloneness. Loneliness and aloneness are starkly different in their impact. As nineteenth-century philosopher Paul Tillich observed: "Our language has wisely sensed the two sides of man's being alone. It has created the word 'loneliness' to express the pain of being alone. And it has created the word 'solitude' to express the glory of being alone." Loneliness depletes life of joy and pleasure; solitude quantitatively infuses these intangibles into life. Loneliness also contains painful elements, such as unhappiness and depression, while aloneness contains tranquil themes of peace and joy and a sense of life's eternal rhythms.

Choose solitude. For solitude to be nourishing, it must be chosen. Being alone doesn't automatically equate to loneliness. Loneliness implies a craving for companionship, a wish not to be alone. Aloneness implies, even in a crowd, *willing* or *choosing* time alone and savoring that time. The challenge, whenever alone, is to transform the discomfort of *loneliness* into a comfortable state of *aloneness with self* and then to enjoy the company. Such an emphatic shift requires centering—a state of generating your own emotional supplies and companionship, of contentedly making yourself company enough.

"Rough it? I'm already roughing it! I'm raising three kids, have a messy husband, and a part-time job!"

"It's the plumber. He wants us to bring the kitchen sink to his shop."

Embrace aloneness. People often flee from solitude, experiencing moments of separation as "loneliness"—not "aloneness." Further, they embrace today's pernicious but erroneous belief that only through relationships can loneliness be quelled. Thus, searching for roots and connections, they depend on others for emotional sustenance and expect them to solve their distress and emptiness. In their misery, they ask, "How can I find someone to cure my loneliness?"

"Just because we're the only two living souls on this planet doesn't mean we have to be friends!"

"I just realized—we forgot to get a phone for us!"

But others can't cure your loneliness. Loneliness can be reduced only within you and by you. You are completely separate from others, ultimately facing life alone. Even in company, you are alone. You may enjoy the society of others, but in quiet, desperate hours you must always return to yourself. Such separateness is inevitable, a fact of the human condition. We are all born alone, discover our life meaning alone, and go to our deaths alone. In your aloneness, your only proactive choice is to abide with yourself with courage, dignity, and peace.

Depend on yourself. Only when you acknowledge your dependence upon yourself for your own emotional well-being can you ask the pertinent questions: How can I convert inevitable loneliness into solitude? and How can I comfortably be alone with myself, perhaps even living and loving alone? Ultimately, your attitude toward being alone determines all, inevitably dictating how you will interpret and experience actual times of separateness.

"We're interested in separate any place!"

"Excuse me, but I believe I had dibs on the office space."

Find self in solitude. Only in solitude can you find your self. Although, as a social creature, you need other people, you need yourself more. In this respect, solitude is inextricably related to the enterprise of maturing. When you're lonely, you're separated from yourself, not from others. And only through self-discovery, eminently attainable in solitude, can you achieve self-integration.

"You must be Adam, and you must be Eve.
I'm George, your insurance agent."

*"You live for the moment? Then how come at this
moment you're not cleaning your room?"*

The magic of solitude, of course, is that you can become reacquainted with your self. With others absent, you can spontaneously focus on your own solitary presence. You can directly access your deeper spirit. You can experience infinite inner harmony with an infinite outer universe. You can risk moving in new directions to find your own unique life path. You can cultivate self-refinement and a growing sense of identity. And you can become more complete and live a richer, fuller life.

*"I sure thought they'd take the hint and go home
when we said we were going to bed."*

Strengthen relationships. Although intimate relationships are an axis around which life revolves, relationships are only one axis. Another axis, this in juxtaposition, is the axis of being by or with oneself. Intimacy with others rests in the context of these two axes, rooted in the emotional ebb and flow of being together and being apart.

Ultimately, solitude allows you to feel your distinctive separateness from others, a necessary counterpoint to intimacy. Without solitude, incidentally, intimacy would have no reference point or meaning. Choosing solitude provides soul-restoring nourishment and helps you prepare to renew relationships. In return, you are potentially more centered, more focused, and more sophisticated regarding the affairs of your relationships. Finally, through self-reflection you can more easily share your inner self and thus form deeper intimate relationships.

Rejuvenate. Solitude ministers to subtle forms of emotional exhaustion, offering absolute respite from harsh daily stimulation. Solitude is thus a healing balm unlike any other, a quiet suspension in the river of time.

"It sounds like they're moving furniture against the door."

Be still. The stillness and serenity of solitude slow the heartbeat, lower the blood pressure, and make things ultimately more workable and enjoyable. As well, the stillness of solitude brings stillness of spirit. Such stillness may bring insight or enlightenment as sudden answers or intuitive realizations spontaneously spring into consciousness.

"Thank you for allowing us to examine your soul. Unfortunately, however, your soul does not meet our needs at this time. Best of luck in placing it elsewhere."

"Yes?"

Seek soul. Your soul is constant, ever present, and ever available for access in solitude, the realm where the soul resides. However, preoccupied with superficial pursuits, you may inadvertently obscure the pathway to "soul," to that deeper inner consciousness of an eternal nature. In the calmness of solitude, however, you can readily reconnect with your soul by simply shifting your consciousness inward. And because the pathways to self and soul are congruous, you can momentarily wed mind and spirit.

"Please move along, sir—you're depressing the hyena."

"And this is my sentimental favorite.
It's the last video my husband shot!"

Give absolute attention. Momentarily paying absolute
attention is a means of deeply experiencing your spiritual
center. Even the most commonplace of natural objects—a
flower, a tree, a stone—promises something miraculous.
Therefore, give absolute attention to the minute wonders sur-
rounding you, even revere those wonders. In so doing, you
will enter the realm of the exquisite and the realm of the

"Haven't you found your cubicle yet?"

Creator. And when in that realm you lose yourself, you'll find evidence of Him.

Loaf. Revert to clock-free time and occasionally down-shift from doing to being. Watch the clouds, feel raindrops falling, or listen to the sound of flowing streams. Walk aimlessly in the woods or along the beach shores. Eat when you're hungry. Rest when you're tired. Leave your watch at home. In the present moment, simply enjoy the wondrous rapture of being.

Let nature heal. Communion with nature is perhaps your most forceful potential de-stressor and your greatest restorative source. The natural rhythms of nature—the assurance that dawn triumphs over night and spring after winter—offer a soul-touching intangible that is lasting, substantive, and infinitely healing. Those ever in admiration and awe of nature are never weary of life. Nor do they lack enduring strength. In her diary, Anne Frank astutely observed: "The best remedy for those who are afraid, lonely or unhappy is to go outside, somewhere where they can be quite alone with the heavens, nature and God . . . nature brings solace in all troubles."

CHAPTER 20

Engineer Your Life

You can take measures to eliminate, control, or diminish various conditions or events that invariably push your stress buttons. You can also create conditions or events that further your life and life satisfaction. From below, then, consider possible ways to engineer your life. First consider ways of dealing with today's overwhelming and intrusive technology.

Control noise levels. It's no secret that noise causes stress. And noise can damage hearing and affect health. Thus, muffle sound in work and living space. Keep the noisiest appliances away from living areas. Avoid loud, glaring, and intensive noises. And, of course, refrain from being a noisemaker yourself.

"But I have tried prayer!"

"So, this is what started the whole thing . . ."

Reduce information overload. We live in the Information Age. Every day you probably struggle through a jungle of data and a tangle of phone messages, faxes, e-mails, computer printouts, and no end of media dot coms. You have to sort through the din of talk shows, all-day news broadcasts, the latest stock-market updates, and books and magazines about everything, anything, and nothing. You further deal with "brand clutter," forcing you to make choices between literally dozens or hundreds of personal and household products.

"You're a workaholic, Mr. Baxter. You'll have to leave your beeper with me!"

As a result, your brain sometimes shorts out and shuts down. The only truly healthy life approach is to institute strong counter-measures that provide your brain intervals of relief. You can create such respite by setting aside times to turn off the information flow. You can severely restrict the amount of information you print or store. And daily you can seek momentary refuges of solitude and serenity from all that churns and besets your minds, even at times retreating for renewal to a park, a museum, or a house of worship.

"Ms. Carol Webster is here for her audit."

Regulate television. Most people say they don't have enough "time." Yet, too often, too much "time" is frivolously spent in front of a television. Weighing television time against time allocated to our heart's priorities might shock us into reassessing and re-prioritizing. Frankly, most of us could make more "time" for heartfelt affairs by watching less TV. And often, less TV equals less stress.

This does not represent an argument against television, but against watching *just anything* on television. Some television programs are senseless—essentially junk food for the mind. Worse is endless programming that elevates depravity rather than morality. David Frost said: "Television permits you to be entertained in your living room by people you wouldn't have in your home."

Unregulated television watching can also cause stress. Admittedly, TV can be relaxing, entertaining, and educational. TV can also be highly addictive, leading to passive lifestyles that generate low life-satisfaction. All this to say: take charge of the television.

"OK, you may leave the room!"

Moderate your viewing time. Be selective of programs. And balance TV time against your truest life priorities. We all have a deep-seated need to find in life the genuine and the enduring. In this respect, an inordinate preoccupation with TV or any state-of-the-art technology can interfere with matters of the soul.

Relinquish hurry. Harassed by the clock, you probably hurry and scurry to achieve your purposes. But to what end? Most often, that end is simply to achieve other purposes, and then even others, continuing ad infinitum in a relentless and futile pursuit of a finish line. There is no stopping place, no line drawn in the sand, no sign informing, "That's enough."

"The only thing we had in your price range just collapsed!"

"Hurry" is a pestilent affliction of mankind not restricted to our own millennium. In a classic essay, written nearly a century ago, and in words keenly apropos to today, William George Jordan wrote: "Hurry has ruined more Americans than has any other word in the vocabulary in life. It is the scourge of America."

So how can you stop hurrying? To begin with, remind yourself that the entire universe won't grind to a halt if you slow down. To moderate your sense of urgency, distinguish between necessary haste (being on time for an appointment) and mere impatience (waiting restlessly for a faxed letter). Ruthlessly weed out daily activities, tasks, errands, and events that cause unnecessary hurry. Many things in life can wait. Sometimes phone calls are better returned later, decisions better made tomorrow, and problems better left to simmer a bit.

To reduce urgency, check any tendency to produce without limit. Momentarily ask yourself: Do I really need to rush? Is the consequence of rushing worse than not rushing? Finally, remind yourself that slowing down will help you reclaim the most valuable thing you own: your time.

*"Our retirement plan is quite simple—we buy
you a state lottery ticket every month."*

Spend your time wisely. If you live until age seventy-five—and general life expectancy, now in the mid-eighties, is rapidly increasing—you have 657,000 earth hours to spend. The question, of course, is how to allocate such time judiciously so that you attend to the people you care about, your goals, and yourself. Allocating 657,000 hours carte blanche may be overwhelming, but not so daunting if you allocate your hours day-by-day, week-by-week, or year-by-year. (Some of us actually consciously allocate our minutes.)

"You forgot to say 'when,' Mr. Smith."

Make conscious life choices. Many people lead an unexamined life much of the time. However, daily life offers you an ever-changing mix of givens and choices, and authentic satisfaction comes only from measuring those choices against the counterweights of your deepest values and commitments. Decide then who and what matters most. Perhaps construct a list of ten. Subsequently contemplate, "Does the way I allocate time reflect my true priorities?"

*"I have to go to the bathroom. Do you promise
not to invade my space while I'm gone?"*

Designate your life purpose. Making wise life choices is predicated upon wisely choosing a life mission. For maximum fulfillment and minimum stress, you must embrace a rewarding and heart-centered life purpose. And only after determining your mission in life (as opposed to how much you can get done), can you fundamentally modify the way you use time.

Follow your life purpose. Mega-stress and unhappiness can result from just meandering through life, not getting a grip, not deciding where you're going. However, with a lifestyle rich in purpose, you can give directed attention to planning both your life and time. And always, a fruitful life mission emerges when you invest in a worthy and enduring cause that promises to outlast you.

"Does it come with a seat belt? I have a tendency to fall asleep."

No matter how old you get, you still have something to offer the universe. At any age, life's greatest satisfaction always lies in knowing your life counts; that you stand for something that matters; and that the world is a bit better for your being in it. And, to the extent that you achieve a designated life mission, you will likely address life's most persistent overarching question, "What am I doing for others?"

"I know, I know! This is the only thing I didn't consider!"

"Don't laugh! We haven't been robbed since I built it!"

Sculpt your life. Throughout your life you are shaping your own soul. To view yourself in a clearer perspective and to explore the potential bounty of your life, consider these penetrating questions:

- If dreams could come true, what would you wish for?

- If someone dropped a million dollars in your lap, would you be in the same job (career, profession) tomorrow?

- What would you do if you were allotted two extra hours a day?

- How would you allocate time differently if each hour were worth one thousand dollars?

- If you knew you would die next Monday, what would you do this weekend?

- If you did die next Monday, to whom would you want to say good-bye? Express regrets? Ask for forgiveness? Express your love?

- If you were to give more generously to

others, even help a little to reduce the world's misery, what would you do?

- If you had a near-death experience, how would that experience change your life, influence your commitment to a life purpose, or change any quest for the spiritual and divine?

- If you were to invest more time and energy in your self and soul, what would you do?

- If, purportedly, you could speak to your guardian angel, what would you say? What might you request? In what direction would you like your guardian angel to guide you?

Invest in invaluable self. All the preceding questions address the issue of furthering your intellectual, emotional, and spiritual self. You were born with a unique set of abilities, backgrounds, passions, and potentials. And with these materials, you're on an endless quest of becoming—of creating with your own chisel your own masterpieces.

"Do you have a model that he won't have to warm up while I get the kids ready?"

"That's right, sir, no collateral is necessary. However, we will have to chain this little electronic device around your neck!"

As an invaluable and irreplaceable human being, you're well worth your own investment. You are, in essence, a soul of divine origin spiritually created by God himself. You are thus intrinsically valuable simply because you are. You are a miracle of immeasurable proportions, a marvel in the universe. As such a precious being, acknowledge who you are, celebrate your invaluable self, and applaud your potential. Then pursue that potential. Discover the ways you're exceptional and then maximize your endowments. Celebrate who you divinely are within God's eternal creations.

Make someone happy. Consider the abundant life contribution should you daily make someone happy. In ten years you could make 3,650 persons happy—that's equivalent to the population of a small town. Happily, when you make someone happy, you increase *your* happiness quotient. Each time you enlarge another's life, the universe— giving back in like measure—enlarges your own.

Make yourself happy. By momentarily savoring life's little things, happiness is delightfully within your reach. And those little things seem limitless: Laughing with someone you like. A friend at the door. Two socks that match. Finding your car keys. A cool drink on a hot day. Five green traffic lights in a row. Any refund. And incomprehensible good luck.

"Then one day the electric bill, the heating bill, the water bill, real estate taxes, and our Christmas shopping bills all came together."

These little things, little hinges of the universe, count a lot. And, if you fine-tune your perceptions, you will notice that such little hinges pleasantly pique your sense of well-being. It follows then, that as you increasingly delight in little things, you increasingly enrich your life and insure your happiness.

"Bad case of scheduling—seems he had too many stress management seminars for one day."

CHAPTER 21

Count Your Blessings

In today's world, blessings are everywhere. They are incalculable gifts of comfort, convenience, and sustenance. With such endowments, we all should feel nothing but simple, humble reverence and gratitude—two profound conditions that preclude the stressing of soul. Nothing is more soothing to soul, in fact, than fully comprehending that we have a loving Creator who, in his love, endowed us with incomprehensible and miraculous blessings. Here then, consider ways to heighten your consciousness of those infinite blessings:

"At last! Someone who understands our new tax laws!"

"It may be small, but it will give you that big car feeling."

Revere your existence. Consider the supreme blessing of just *being*. We should all be profoundly amazed that we even exist, as expressed by Henry David Thoreau: "I have never gotten over my surprise that I should have been born in the most [enviable] place in the world, and in the very nick of time."

*"Before you begin looking at athletic shoes, perhaps
you should speak with our loan officer?"*

"Is Thanksgiving over?"

Venerate abundance. Consider your boundless abundance. A hundred years ago your every personal possession would have been considered a miracle, not just a blessing. Today you enjoy more blessings at the millennium's turn than have the combined total of all your predecessors throughout time. Remember then that you are gifted with not entitled to your earthly sustenance.

"I say this place is fast!"

"I hope and pray they're making a movie."

Acclaim wonders. Many blessings consist of wonders you may take for granted, wonders that fifty years ago would have awed people beyond measure: home air conditioning, frozen foods, anti-polio vaccines, automatic washers, the computer, the Internet, modern medical miracles.

"I don't know what he removed during surgery—
he keeps telling me it's none of my business!"

Cherish family. Among your profound blessings is the family, with its inherent ties to people who love and support you. Families represent security, assuring that someone cares whether you are alive and well on this planet.

"Cynthia and her children are accustomed to all the comforts of home, so I suggested we live here after we're married."

"OK, talk—I counted all my blessings and there's one missing!"

Treasure children. Another profound blessing is a child—the heart's most precious treasure. The health or safety of a child for even a day is an infinite gift. Asked to donate to a family who lost a child, a husband protested privately to his wife: "Why should we give money? It wasn't our child." Responded his wife: "We should give money because it *wasn't* our child."

"Are we glad to hear that you don't know where you'll get the money you need—for a minute there we were afraid you wanted to get it from us."

Rejoice in home. Home is the place that harbors the people you love. It is a place where childhood memories abound, a place of permanence where a scrawny dog with a high-frequency tail frantically greets you while the observing cat looks slightly less bored.

When you're far away and lonely, there's nothing like home. And when you're home, no food is so good as that you eat with your feet tucked under your own table.

Laud your health. Without the blessing of health, quality of life potentially may be diminished to zero—and all the world's money cannot restore that blessing.

Revere freedom. Never forget the blessing of residing in a democracy that assures freedom from tyranny. Things may not always seem perfect, and social ills still need correcting, but this country guarantees your right to be who you are, where you are.

"You don't have to wait for a 'beep' to give God a message."

Give gratitude. Finally, in counting your infinite blessings, give gratitude to your Creator. Do so humbly, with a cheerful heart. Consider the actions of Joseph Haydn, an eighteenth-century Austrian composer, who had been criticized in church for his music's gaiety. Haydn responded to his critics: "I cannot help it. I give forth what is in me. When

I think of the Divine Being, my heart is so full of joy that the notes fly off as from a spindle. And as I have a cheerful heart, He will pardon me if I serve him cheerfully."

As with Joseph Haydn, our own gratitude can "fly off as from a spindle," permeating and stirring heart and soul. As we joyously savor God's creations and works, a consummate life blessing comes in simply knowing just whom to thank.

Sources

Allen, Gladys, organizational expert. Personal conversations with author, 1999.

Astaire, Fred, screen test, as quoted in *The Little Brown Book of Anecdotes,* Clifton Fadiman, ed. (Boston: Little, Brown and Co., 1985), 24.

Beebee, William, and Roosevelt Theodore, in Allen Klein, *The Healing Power of Humor* (Los Angeles: J. P. Tarcher, 1989), 12.

Bendfelt, Vicki, in *Quote Magazine,* 18 February 1962, 15.

Borkovec, Thomas, "What's the Use of Worrying," *Psychology Today,* December 1985, 59.

Bowring, John, as quoted in Bill Kirby, "Postcard Collection Near Done," *The Augusta Chronicle,* 25 July 1997, B1.

Carrington, Patricia, *Releasing* (New York: William Morrow and Company, Inc., 1984), 46–58.

Carver, George Washington, as quoted in Lawrence Elliott, *George Washington Carver: The Man Who Overcame* (Englewood Cliffs, N. J.: Prentice Hall, Inc. 1966), 195–96.

Cohen, Sherry Suib, "The Giggle Factor," *New Woman,* March 1989, 39.

Cosby, Bill, *Love and Marriage* (New York: Doubleday, 1989), 147.

Dunne, Harry P., *One Question That Can Save Your Marriage* (New York: Perigree Books, 1991), 27.

Dyer, Wayne, *Your Erroneous Zones* (New York: Funk and Wagnalls, 1976), 126.

Frank, Anne, *The Diary of a Young Girl* (New York: Doubleday, 1952), 184.

Frost, David, as quoted in *Newsweek,* 5 March 1990, 54.

Greyling, Dan P., in *Reader's Digest,* July 1980, 21.

Hall, Donald, *Principal Products of Portugal* (Boston: Beacon Press, 1995), 65.

Haydn, Joseph, as quoted in Catherine Drinker, *Biography: The Craft and the Calling* (Boston: Little, Brown and Company, 1968), 148.

Jordan, Paul and Margaret, *Do I Have to Give up Me to Be Loved by You?* (New York: KJF Books, 1983), 7–10.

Jordan, William George, *Self-Control: Its Kingship and Majesty* (New York: Fleming H. Revell Company, 1905), 115.

Landers, Ann, in Anne P. Stern, "The Feeling We Can't Live Without," *McCall's,* November 1992, 84.

McLaughlin, Mignon, as quoted in "The Neurotic's Notebook," *The Atlantic Monthly,* July 1964, 119.

Noyes, Marilyn, as quoted in Carma Wadley, "Having It All? Myths, Illusions, Realities," *Deseret News,* 25 April 1994, C1.

Phelps, William Lyon, *Happiness* (New York: E. P. Dutton & Co., 1935), 43.

Ridenour, Fritz, *The Marriage Collection* (Grand Rapids, Mich.: Zondervan Publishing House, 1989), 512.

Romano, Catherine, as quoted in Ron Alexander, "Metropolitan Diary," *New York Times,* 13 March 1991, C2.

Signoret, Simone, in Robert Andrews, ed., *Columbia Dictionary of Quotations* (New York: Columbia University Press, 1993), 561.

Thomas, Lewis, *The Lives of a Cell* (New York: Penguin Books, 1974), 85.

Thoreau, Henry David, as quoted in Dean Noit, ed., *Inspired Words for the Inspired Life* (Chicago: C. A. Welch and Co., 1909), 226.

Tillich, Paul, as quoted in Clark E. Moustakas, *Loneliness and Love* (Englewood Cliffs, N. J.: Prentice-Hall, Inc., 1972), 49–50.

Twain, Mark, *Man Is the Only Animal That Blushes . . . Or Needs To: The Wisdom of Mark Twain* (New York: Random House, 1970), 53.

Wilson, Flip, as quoted in Dale Turner, "Gifts That Cost Nothing Can Make the World Richer," *Seattle Times,* 7 December 1996, C4.

Wilson, Woodrow, as quoted in William C. Rhoden, "Sports of the Times," *The New York Times,* 1 December 1999, D1.